MACRAMÉ KNOTS AND PATTERNS FOR BEGINNERS

The Ultimate Guide to Learn Macramé
with Step-by-Step Projects.
Discover How Easily You Can Decorate Your Home and
Create Unique Handmade Accessories

Eva Thompson

Table of Contents

Introduction

The art of macramé has been around for centuries, and while the techniques have evolved, the basic premise remains the same. With just a few simple knots, you can create beautiful pieces of art that will stun your guests.

Macramé is the perfect way to add a personal touch to your home, and with so many different knots and designs to choose from, you can create a composition that is uniquely you. So, whether you want to add some extra décor to your home or garden, macramé is the perfect option.

The first time I ever saw a macramé project was in a magazine many years ago. It was a beautiful wall hanging with colorful beads woven throughout. I was intrigued by the project but never took the time to learn how to do it myself.

Some time ago, I asked my grandmother if she knew macramé, and she told me that her mother used to make them all the time; then she showed me some of the pieces her mother had made, and I was amazed at the intricate designs. So, when she taught me how to do macramé, I knew I had found a new passion.

After a bit of practice, I found that the knots and stitches used in macramé were simpler than I expected. Consequently, I started impressing my loved ones with the beautiful pieces I was able to make. Many years have passed since that day, but even now, I feel a sense of satisfaction and pride when I complete a project.

Some might say that macramé is just a bunch of knots, but to me, it is a delicate and beautiful art form. Each piece is unique and tells a story. Plus, it is a great way to relax and de-stress after a long day. I think that's why macramé is so popular. It is an accessible form of art that anyone can do, and the results are stunning.

If you are looking for a new hobby, macramé is an excellent option. You will discover that it is easy to learn, inexpensive, and versatile. Plus, it is relaxing and makes a great gift.

This book is designed to teach you the basic knots of macramé. Once you have a handle on the basics, you will be able to start experimenting with some different designs and patterns and create your firsts own stunning pieces. But, then, there are endless possibilities for macramé, so let your imagination run wild.

Macramé could be a great way to make a living, especially if you are talented in creating beautiful and unique designs. There are many opportunities for work in the macramé industry, such as starting your own small business, becoming a teacher, or selling your creations online or in stores. With the right skills and creativity, you can live well with macramé.

So why not give it a try? Continue reading and start learning the art of macramé!

What is Macramé?

History of Macramé

Macramé is a textile art that consists of natural materials such as hemp, cotton twine, linen, leather, jute, or yarn for knotting and hitching. Macramé has been reborn today by art enthusiasts who want to work using their hands. Macramé is all around us. In a yoga class devoted to demonstrating to you how to weave something together knotty hanging for the wall, a plant hanger drapery, or a tiny key chain, you may not have to search much for a workshop. Boho and minimalist blends allow for a warm yet trendy look.

In opposition to knitting or weaving, Macramé is a form of textile produced by knotting strategies. The knots create full-hitch as well as double half-hitches and are square. Only affordable and available materials such as hemp, leather, cotton twine, or yarn are needed for the craft, with different beads often used to complement the item. This is achieved by hand, avoiding needles, weaving cords or strings together into basic or complicated knots.

The name "macramé" derives from the Ottoman word "mahrama" (or "makrama"), which described both a towel and a headdress handkerchief. In turn, the Ottomans took this term from the Arabs, perhaps from the word "mahramatun" (handkerchief) or "migramah" (decorated fringe). Macramé's development and spread are attributed to 13th-century Arabs who used additional thread-made materials to make knotted festive threads.

However, in China in the third century AD, ceremonial fabrics or wall decorations were made by intertwining ropes and threads with Pan Chang knots knit into infinity patterns to signify durability. These pieces of works are very similar to those used today to make macramé jewelry.

According to one theory, the art of macrame was imported to the West by Genoese sailors. These sailors, during the long hours of navigation, delighted in using this weaving technique to create a series of ornaments and artifacts, then used as a bargaining chip when the sailors arrived at their destination. Sailors utilized the knots even to mesmerize up their weapons, bottles, and pieces of the ship, becoming a big part of the craft's origins. However, their understanding of various styles of knots was being used to exchange intel. As macramé became a standard textile that transformed into placemats, tassels, plant slings, photo frames, wall hangings, and hammocks, the 70s made the ornate string art mainstream.

The art of macrame seemed to have fallen out of use after the 1970s but has recently made a strong comeback in DIY YouTube videos and blogger websites.

Apartment owners discover macramé, especially appealing for its opportunity to modify the several hanging indoor plants across their room as a reply to the shortage of a yard, as well as an implies for having brought the outside in with even more houses springing up as well as trees getting cut down.

Over the last few years, Macramé has been common again, and there are more than fifty kinds of different ties. The Indian braid, chevron, zigzag, diagonal, overhand, stopper knot, double and single braid, infinite knot, a half knot, square knot, among others, are several instances of macramé knots.

Five Ways Macramé Will Help You De-Stress and Have Fun

It is Easy to Learn: With just a few simple knots, you can create beautiful macramé pieces. Plenty of online tutorials and books are available to help you get started. With just a little bit of practice, soon enough, you'll be creating beautiful pieces from the comfort of your own home.

It is Inexpensive: All you need to start is some rope or cord and a pair of scissors. You can find these items at your local crafting store or online. Most projects can be completed in an afternoon with minimal cost. This makes it great for beginners who want to experiment with this craft without investing in expensive tools or materials.

It is Versatile: One of the best things about macramé is it's incredibly versatile. Macramé can be used to create a variety of pieces, from wall hangings, plant hangers, and baskets to necklaces, bracelets, and earrings. You can try different colors of cord or rope to create a wide range of patterns and designs. You can also mix and match different knots to create unique pieces that are all your own and furnish them with beads, rings, and many other items. Once you get the hang of it, the possibilities are endless.

It is Relaxing: The repetitive motions involved in knotting can be calming and meditative. Working on a macramé project has been known to help reduce stress levels, allowing you to step away from your daily life for a while and focus on something creative instead. Working on something creative like this also boosts concentration levels and problem-solving skills. Plus, you'll have something beautiful to show off once you finish your project.

It Makes a Great Gift: Anything created using macrame will surely make someone feel happy and loved. Handmade gifts are always appreciated, and what could be more thoughtful than a macramé piece made just for someone special?

Macramé Materials and Tools

As I told you in the introduction, starting your journey with macramé can be easy and very inexpensive.

In fact, all you really need are four basic tools:

1. Macramé Cord
2. A Cutting tool (like a pair of scissors)
3. A Measuring tool (usually a tape measure)
4. Something to mount your work from (as a ring, a stick or a dowel)

Any kind of cord will do for macramé, but some are better than others. Natural fibers like cotton or hemp are popular choices because they're strong and easy to work with. However, synthetic materials like nylon or polyester can be used as well.

The essential thing is to choose a cord that is thick enough to hold its shape but not so thick that it's difficult to knot. In the next paragraphs, I will describe you what are the differences between them and the best beginner's strings to try.

As for cutting tools, a sharp pair of scissors will do the job just fine. You'll need them to cut the cord to the desired length and shape.

Finally, you'll need a measuring tool to help you achieve precise knots and patterns. A ruler, yardstick, or tape measure will work well.

All you need now is something to mount your work from. A ring, dowel, or cord will do nicely. And that's really all there is to it!

Once you have your four basic macramé tools, you're ready to start creating. With just a few simple supplies, you can start making beautiful macramé creations of your own.

But if you want to go big or get creative with your macrame, in the following paragraph are a few other supplies you might consider adding to your toolkit.

Tools Required for Macramé

Macramé Project Board

A project mounting board is a helpful tool for macramé. The board is the working area where you secure your work. You can find boards with grid-inch markings and fitting directions written on the fronts at art shops. A project board may, therefore, be rendered by gluing together or using cork foam sheets. A board is suitable for a macramé project as long as it is thick enough to prevent the pins from sticking out the back.

T-Pins

T-Pins are used to secure the macramé yarn or rope onto the mounting board. They are also great for holding the fabric in place while you finish a section. T-pins come in various sizes. Smaller pins are ideal for smaller, more delicate designs. Pins will probably break after prolonged use. Those built of steel are more durable and can last longer. The cross-pins method seen here is a perfect way to use pins to lock delicate ropes without damaging them.

Ruler

For measuring purposes, you'll need a ruler, yardstick or tape measure, used to determine the length of the cords you will need for your project, to mark the points at which you will need to make cuts and to ensure all of your knots are even and consistent throughout the project. Measuring is key when it comes to creating macrame patterns.

Pattern

Many things can be created with macramé, from purses to clothes, though you will need a macramé template. Macramé patterns provide step-by-step guidance on the knots used, directions for calculating, and final assembly guidelines. Buy patterns, or you search for them online.

Scissors

A decent pair of sharp scissors will be used to cut threads correctly on a macramé layout. There are different sizes and comfort grips. I prefer large sharp scissors—like the Fiskars scissors. They are 24cm long dress creators' scissors and they are extremely sharp, so please be careful when you use them. In any case, even

6mm yarn gets cut up speedy with these. You can use a special cutter designed specifically for macramé cord too, that will help you to create clean and sharp edges.

Tweezers

Tweezers can be handy for many things, such as undoing knots and sewing on fine thread. I use mine primarily when working with very subtle strings. In these cases, when I have done my knot, it gets pretty tight as well, so if I get it wrong, it's harder to undo it with my fingers; so, using tweezers with a fine tip can be helpful when you are trying not to damage the thread. and the final work.

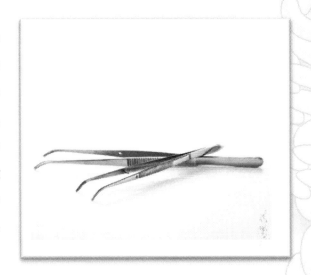

Needles

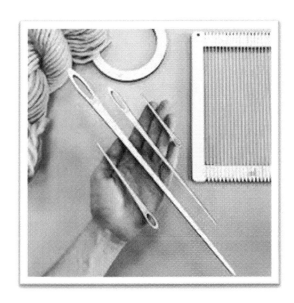

Needles are used in macramé to clean up the completed work and close it. Macramé needles have larger eyes than usual. Depending on the project, can be used use plastic or metallic needles of different sizes. Specific measurements are used to fit yarn styles like silk or nylon and to insert beads in the project.

Tape

Tape it is also handy and can be kept alongside the other macramé materials. You could put tape on the cords' end to keep them from twisting, to mark some point of the project or keep together the strips. You can evaluate buying a cellophane roll and a packing tape dispenser gun that seals packages and makes them more waterproof, just in case you begin selling and delivering your artwork.

Fabric Glue

It is easy to use fabric glue for painting and planning, so make sure to have some handy. Make sure the adhesive dries transparent. You could put glue on the cords' ends of some type fabric to keep them from twisting.

Decoration

Beads, pendants, and clasps for micro-macramé might also be required. As well as macramé beads, circles, animal eyes, and other objects.

Macramé Cords

Today many macrame cords fibers of different thicknesses and colors are available on the market.

Macramé craft creators make use of different types of materials. The materials can be classified in two significant ways: natural and synthetic.

Natural fibers are made from plants and animals, including jute, hemp, leather, cotton, silk, and flax.

The fibers of synthetic materials are made through chemical processes. As natural materials, synthetic materials are also used in macramé projects. The most common are nylon beading cord, olefin, satin cord, and parachute cord.

The term "macrame cord" comprises all types of fibers used for the craft, natural and synthetic, including rope, yarn, string, braided cord, and waxed options.

The word "cord" is often used in macrame patterns, but you can choose any fabric you want. Make sure it is the same thickness throughout, as that will influence the cord you need.

A macramé cord's thickness (or intensity) depends primarily on its structure. For example, jute, ribbon leather, and nylon cord are generally more robust than cotton.

The cord's intensity is calculated by whether the material's specific strands were braided or twisted throughout the manufacturing phase.

In the following paragraphs, I will list the main types of fibers used for macrame projects and explain how to prepare the cords before starting any project.

Difference Between Rope, String, Yarn, and Braided Cord

Macramé rope

This is typically a 3-strand cotton cord where the fibers are wrapped around each other (sometimes called a 3-ply). You may find it in four strands, but the traditional rope will be three.

Macramé rope is usually stronger and thicker than other macramé cords, and it gives you a lovely, wavy fringe when you untwist it, so it is perfect for adding dimension to your job.

Since it is heavier, I like to use it for parts of items that carry considerable weight. Cotton rope is soft enough to be cozy but strong enough to keep knots well. It won't start untwisting in the middle of your project, like some single-strand alternatives.

Polypropylene (or polyolefin) macramé rope is perfect for outdoor usage because it does not lose shape as quickly as cotton.

Unfortunately, macramé rope often stretches when cut, so it will even stretch up depending on where you stay and how much humidity you have so that the edges can look "frizzy," and that's the only thing to keep in mind.

The tightly woven cotton macramé rope is sometimes called "sash rope." Sash rope is slightly rigid and quite hard to remove, yet it is excellent, so it is perfect for weight-bearing parts and if you're trying to add plenty of strength to your job. In my experience, macramé rope is the worst on hands, but you must deal with the slight discomfort when you want a particular look or versatility.

Macramé string

A string is a single-twist smooth unplied cord of fiber thinner than thread. It can be made of natural materials like cotton or hemp or synthetic options like nylon.

A string is one of the most commonly used macrame cord types, especially for micro macrame and small projects.

String stretches faster than thread because it unwinds quickly so that the total width will range from 1 to 3,5 or 9 mm, from when firmly wounded along the conduit to when splitting and breathable.

Yarn: Although usually employed for knitting or weaving, yarn can also serve as a material for macrame. Yarn can be either one single or multiple strands twisted together(plied and unplied) and is most commonly made from wool.

I suggest unplied macrame yarn for softer objects like rugs and baskets. However, it is too soft for wall hangings or plants hangers.

Braided Macramé Cord

This is typically a 6-strand (or more) **braided thread** created by intertwining 6-10 fibers forming a cord. These types of cords are really robust and won't unravel or fray, so they are a good option for outdoor projects, as they are weather-resistant. Unfortunately, it is difficult to unwind this cord to create a "fringe."

Therefore, the cord's ends are often handled before starting a macramé task to avoid splitting.

If you intend to build a fringe with this cord, ensure that the threads don't unravel beyond the fringe's length by knotting the upper part of the fringe.

Some cords of macramé sound rough, and the skin can be irritated. For making necklaces and bracelets, metallic and hemp, use silk, cotton, satin rayon, and nylon; you may still use leather because, in time, it softens.

"What's the right macramé string for beginners?"

It depends on many factors: the nature of the project, where and how the final piece will be, and the crafter's experience. Generally, for a beginner, I will recommend a 5 mm natural cotton string for four main reasons: it is the right size to hang on a nice medium-sized wall, and it fits better than the 3 mm; it has a very compact medium twist on it, and finally, it can be gently unknotted and reknitted a couple of times before losing its elasticity as long as you are careful. And being gentle on the hands, of course, always tends to keep you moving.

Cord Measurement

Macramé cord thickness is generally represented in millimeters (mm). Remember it whether they will be put into buttons, beads, or other decorative items while purchasing a cord.

Strings thick between 4 and 9 millimeters in diameter may need bigger decorations and are mainly used to produce medium or big projects, like wall hangings, runners, coasters or baskets.

For producing micro-macramé items, like earrings, necklaces and bracelets a good-sized string should have a diameter of 2-5 millimeters.

Some cords are available in big rolls, while others appear in shorter lengths.

For any macrame project, it's essential to select the right cord size and accurately determine how many strings you need and their length.

Macrame books and courses usually list the amount of string and the cord length needed to complete their projects.

The cord total amount should be relating to the cord length needed for the whole project. This includes knowing the required cord's length and the total quantity of materials you must purchase.

To measure your cords, you will need paper for writing, a pencil, a tape ruler, and a calculator. You would also need some basic knowledge of unit conversion, as shared below:

- 1 inch = 25.4millimeters = 2.54 centimeters

- 1 foot =12 inches = 30 centimeters

- 1 yard = 3 feet = 36 inches = 90 centimeters

- 20 inches=1,7 feet=50 centimeters

- 40 inches = 3,3 feet=1 meters

- 200 inches = 17 feet=5 meters

Tip: The circumference of a ring = 3.14 * diameter measured across the ring

How to Determine the Number of Strings needed for a Macrame Project and their Length

Do you have an inspiring Macrame project that catches your eye, but you need to know how much string and length is needed to complete it? With some simple guidelines and helpful hints, you can easily approximate the material requirements so that you can make your original masterpieces.

The first thing to do is determine the finished width of the widest area of your project.

Once you have this width, pencil it down.

The most common rule to calculate the number of strings required to create your project is to **divide the project's width by the cord's diameter (in centimeters) x3.**

For example, If you chose a macrame cord with a diameter of 3mm to do a project with a final width of 45 cm, making a little math you will calculate:

$$45 / (0.3 \times 3) = 50$$

Therefore, you will need 50 double ropes (folded in half) or 25 single ropes to make your macrame piece.

Remember though that number can fluctuate depending on whether spacing is close together or spread out; also keep in mind that when picking cord sizes bigger typically means wider space between each strand.

Once you determine the size of your project and the number of wires, you will be able to calculate the length of cord required.

Before calculating the length of macrame rope you need, there are some essential logical criteria to keep in mind:

- The greater the diameter of the string, the greater its length.

- The more knots there are, the more string you need.
- The tighter the knots you tie, the more length of cord you must use.

You can set three simple rules:

- If your project has **loose knots** or **lace patterns**, you must **multiply by four** the final length of the project (the longest stitch).
- If your piece is formed of **tight knots**, you must **multiply by five** the final length of the project.
- If you must use **complex knots**, the design size will be **multiplied by six**.

For example: for an 80cm long piece, which you want to make with 3mm diameter ropes, you will need 80 x 4 = 320 cm or 3.20 m for each string. And therefore, 3.20 x 50 = 160 m of rope in total.

If your cords are folded in half: 80 x 8 = 640 cm or 6.40 m for each string. That is 6.40 x 50 = 320 m of rope in total, plus a few centimeters for the lark's head knots that will be used to hang your macrame on its support.

You must know each knot's width and spacing (if required). You should also determine if you want to add more cords to widen if you need extra cords for damps. With the formulas given above, you can even eventually determine the circumference of the ring for your designs.
Determining the mounting technique is also essential: the cord can be mounted to a dowel, ring, or other cord. Remember, finally, that folded cards affect both the length and width of the cord measurement.

Since you are new to macrame, be always generous with ropes: it's better to have too much yarn than not enough. You will always utilize the extra cord to make a macrame feather or to decorate a flower vase.

While you're learning, getting the length of the rope perfectly can be dangerous. The length of the string needed for a project will vary contingent upon the sort of bunches utilized, the example, the strain of your work, and the rope's component.

It would be best if you never too had too little string since it very well may be confounded to add extra to your piece. I generally recommend you cut on at any rate 10% more than you might suspect you will require as a saver check.

There are bunches of little undertakings to do with your extra rope: you can attempt macramé leaves or a keychain or add the pieces as edges to other works. The alternative is an incomplete project.

Cord Preparation

While usually rarely emphasized, the preparation of cords for projects is one of the fundamental pillars of the art of macramé.

In general, macramé cord preparation is mostly about managing the cut ends and preventing these ends from fraying during the project but sometimes can include some steps of cord conditioning.

During a project, the constant handing of materials can distort the ends, which can have disastrous consequences on your project.

For example, you must adequately pre-treat particular string types, such as those made by twisting individual strands together, so that string doesn't fall apart, effectively destroying your design.

Therefore, cord preparation is extremely and incomparably important to any macramé project's success. The preparation of each cord is meant to be done during the first step, before making any knot, so you cut out your desired cord length from the more significant piece.

It is possible to prevent the ends from fraying through a flame, a knot, tape, and glue.

To avoid the raveling of your cord, using a flame, firstly you must test a small piece of the material with the flame from a small lighter. The material needs to melt, not burn. If it burns, such a cord is unsuitable for flame preparation. To prepare using a flame, hold the cord to the flame's tip for 2 to

5 seconds and make sure the cord does not ignite but melts. Flame preparation is suitable for cords made from olefin, polyester, and nylon, and the process is necessary for parachute cords.

Tape is an economic good way to ensure the end of the cords. Simply apply a piece of tape to the ends of the cords. At the end of the project you could wrap or cut the tape.

Glue is another priceless alternative that can prevent fraying at the ends of cords efficiently. However, not all kinds of glue may be used in cord preparation. Only certain craft glue brands may be used in cord preparation, such as Aleen's Stop Fray. Eventually, you might use household glue, but only when diluted with water. Apply a piece of tape to the ends of the cords, then add some white craft glue only on the last part of them. Ensure that the glue or sealant is dry before taking off the tape; this process should only take a couple hours.

For **cord conditioning**, experts recommend rubbing beeswax along the length of the cord. To condition your cord, get a bit of beeswax, let it warm in your hands, and rub it along its length. This will help prevent unwanted tight curls on your cord.

Note that you may apply beeswax to both natural and synthetic materials. After conditioning, inspect your cords for imperfections and discard useless pieces to ensure your project's perfection.

Preparing your Working Station

Now that I have listed all the materials and tools you might need for your macrame projects, it might all seem a bit overwhelming. For this reason, I will briefly explain how to prepare your workstation and start immersing yourself in the beautiful world of macrame.

You will need just a few more items to get started after you receive your macramé cords.

Standard macramé supplies include cords, a tape ruler, a pair of sharp scissors, pins, and something to start off/mount your work from like a ring, dowel, or cord ; decorations like rings, hooks or beads are often but not always used.

You can make a horizontal or vertical work station, based on your needs and type of macramé project to start.

A horizontal work station could be more comfortable when you choose small or medium size projects with more subtle cords.

The possible supports are many: old corkboards, cardboards, cutting boards, wood's tables, blocking mats for knitting, and so on. I started with a note journal, mounting my cords on a pencil. My favorite is a foam pillow, which I cover with a cloth.

Another choice would be a professional macramé project board. The dimensions of a standard size project board are 11.5 x 15.5 inches and made of a 0.5-inch-thick foam. You can purchase it at most craft stores or websites like Amazon or Etsy.

In any case, it would be better if you had a big enough board piece to set it on your lap and lean against a desk with ease and block the cords and the work you can use some T-pins and tape.

T pins are an essential supply used to keep work on board. Macramé boards are often rectangular, portable, and made of particleboard or cork. T pins penetrate the panels to keep the Macramé project in progress and allow you to work on your project comfortably without any risk of losing your spot or too much movement, which could harm the outcome.

These pins are named around the broad, significant cross-area that makes the pins simple to maneuver.

Make sure you use beautiful, sturdy pins to keep your project pined against your working area; I suggest sewing pins or T-pins that they use to hold wigs fixed on the foam heads. If your cord is delicate, like a satin cord, using the sewing pins with the colored balls on top would be helpful. We are not going to leave a big hole as often do the T-pins.

A vertical macrame workstation is easier to manage when working on large or medium-sized projects with medium or thicker cables, mainly because it prevents ropes from tangling together to create confusion while working on a project.

To assemble a vertical workstation, you can use a dowel, ring, S-hooks, or cord to hang or mount your work on decent adjustable clothes racks, an over the door hanger, or window curtain bars.

A good rule of thumb is that the vertical workstation should be twice as long as the cables you use for the project.

Then, with a larger workspace, you can easily keep the ropes apart and hang them in easy-to-access sections.

About decorations

You can use decorations and other accessories to add extra detail and texture to your projects.

The rings used for macramé projects vary from crucial chain size or small to large hoops. Hoops or loops can also be used as frames so that the vine always joins the nodes attached to it. Copper rings are classical macramé supplies, but steel, wood, and plastic are also popular, although they are less used than copper. Different sizes of rings are available for different projects, such as a top hanger or a bottom point for a bowl.

The shapes of macramé decorations aren't just round—a hoop or frame could be square or heart-shaped in addition to the star, tree, or animal shaped; but despite the different shapes available, the most commonly used are the round rings.

Beads are used in many macramé pieces. These come from wood, ceramic, and plastic. Folk shapes of beads for macramé supplies are round, oval, and cylindrical.
Wood beads can be light or dark in color. Plastic beads used in vineyard projects may be transparent or opaque, while the ceramic macramé beads tend to be ornamented with painted floral motifs.

Five Macramé Tips for Beginners

Practice the Basic Knots

There are a few basic knots that you will need to know to get started with macrame. The half hitch knot and square knot are two of the most commonly used knots, so be sure to practice them until you feel confident. If you are feeling adventurous, try more complex knots like spiral and diamond knots. This will help you get a feel for the material and make sure that your knots are even and tight. The strength with which you fix the knots influences the consistency of their size.

Practice again and again until you discover a musicality and see that your knots will become predictable. You will have to find a balance between trying to lose, having your work look poor, and hitching too tight You can practice on a piece of scrap fabric or rope before moving on to your project. Once you have mastered these basic knots, you can start to create your first projects.

Start with Simple Projects

If you are a beginner, it is best to start with simple projects that only require a few knots. There are many beautiful and complex macrame patterns out there, but they can be difficult to execute if you are a beginner. Stick to something simple until you get the hang of the basics. Once you get the hang of the basic knots, you can move on to more complex projects.

Ask for Help if You Need It

If you get stuck or run into trouble, don't be afraid to ask for help from a friend or family member who is more experienced with macrame. There are also plenty of online forums, YouTube channels, and Facebook groups where you can get advice from other macrame enthusiasts. This is a great way to get answers, ideas, and tips on how to improve your skills.

Take Your Time

Macrame is not a race. Take your time as you work on your project, and enjoy the process. This is an excellent opportunity to relax and unwind after a long day. If you rush, you may make mistakes that will be difficult to fix. Relax and take your time knotting the cord into place to create your beautiful project.

Be Creative and Have Fun

Macrame is a great way to relax and express your creativity, so don't be afraid to. Add your own personal touch and make something that reflects your style. Experiment with different patterns and designs to create a piece of art you will be proud to show off. Most importantly, have fun and enjoy the process. There are no rules, so let your imagination run wild!

Finally, remember that practice makes perfect. With a little bit of patience and practice, you will be able to create beautiful macramé projects in no time.

Basic Macramé Knots

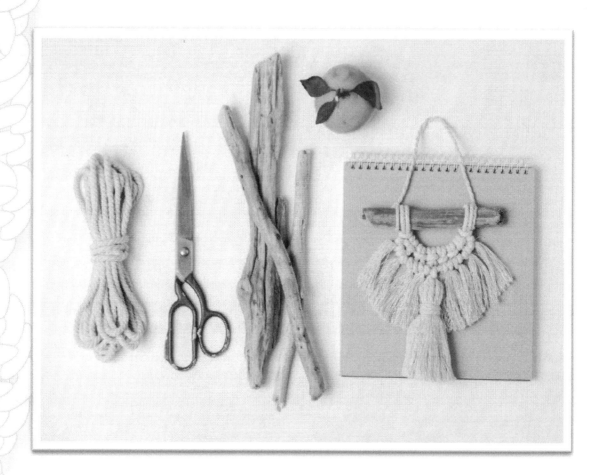

The following knots are excellent starter knots for any project and can be used as a base for many design. Use lightweight cord for this—it can be purchased at craft stores or online wherever you get your macramé supplies. Do not rush and make sure you have even tension throughout. Practice makes perfect, but you won't find it hard to create with the illustrations to help you.

36

Lark's Head Knot (Frivolité Knot)

Instructions:

1. Fold in half your working cord forming a U-shape.

2. Put the loop <u>over and behind the dowel</u>, and, finally,

3. Pull the ends of the chord <u>through</u> the loop and tighten.

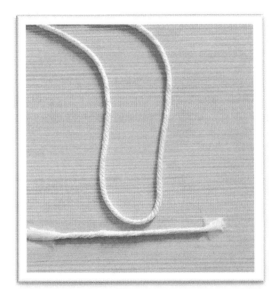 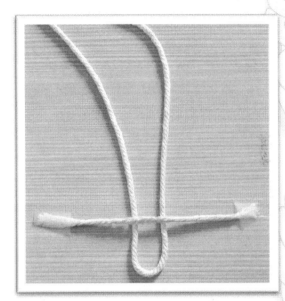

Backwards Lark's Head Knot (Cow Hitch)

As the name implies, this knot is essentially a backward lark's head knot. You can make it by placing your folded in half U-shaped working cord <u>over</u> and <u>in front</u> the dowel and sliding its ends first under the dowel and then into the loop.

Half Hitch Knot

This is one of the most famous macramé knots. It is possible to make it in both directions by switching the cords, but I will show you only one side for brevity.

Instructions:

1. Begin by knotting a Lark's head knot.
2. Bring your left cord over the other to form a 4-shape.
3. Take the end of the left cord and pass it under the other cord.
4. Loop it through the 4-shape and pull it tight. That's it; you just created a half hitch. Below in the picture you can see the execution.

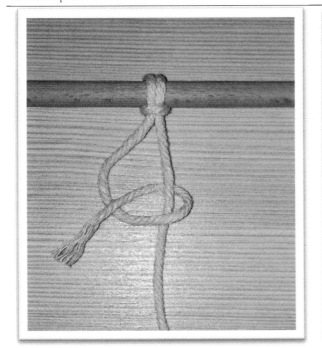

Tip: A spiral half hitch knots can be tied with a sinnet of half hitch knot made in the same direction.

Double Half-Hitch Knot (Clove Hitch Knot)

This knot is made by repeating twice the half-hitch knot: the first Half Hitch Knot is essential to keep the good tension and direction, and the second Half Hitch Knot keeps the first one in place.

Your holding cord must be tight and straight, and make sure to tense your first Half Hitch knot correctly to avoid any gap between your work and the row of knots. If a gap forms, it will get more significant as you go along, so you must go back and fix this before continuing.

This knot can be knitted in three different variations based on the inclination of the leader cord: horizontal, vertical, and diagonal. Point your holding cord always in the direction you want the line to go when you tie on the Double Half Hitch Knots.

Instructions:

1. Begin by knotting three Lark's Head knots.
2. Create a 4-shape using the first one of your left cords (leader cord).
3. Take the second cord (working cord) on the left and loop it <u>over</u> and <u>through</u> the 4-shape, then pull tight.
4. Again, take the second cord on the left and loop it <u>over</u> and <u>through</u> the 4-shape, and pull tight.
5. Repeat the steps 2-4 for all the other working cords to complete the row.

Once the first row is completed, to change direction and begin the next one will be enough to continue with the same leader cord, folding it back on itself and making the knots starting from the opposite side (in these cases, from the right side to the left.)

Tip: To have the end row a bit rounded, take the first filler cord of the new row and again tie a double half-hitch knot as before but this time, instead of lining it up underneath, put it sideways. And then, tie the second filler string in the new direction.

In the next pages, you can see the step-by-step pictures for all three types of Double Hitch Knot.

Horizontal Double Hitch Knot

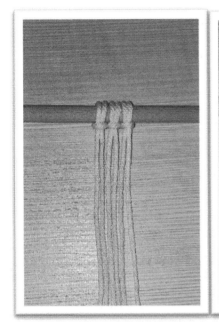

Diagonal Double Hitch Knot

Vertical Double Hitch Knot

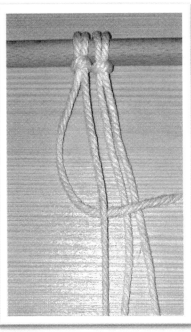

Square Knot

The main characteristic of a square knot is its two fundamental parts. The half square is often known as its first part, while the other part produces a complete square knot upon completion.

This is how to go about it:

1. Start by making two Lark's Head knots. In the end, you will have four macramé cords.
2. Pick the external left cord and get it over the other three ropes, forming a 4-shape.
3. Pick up the external right cord and place it on top of the left cord's end and under the two-center cords.
4. Then to complete the knot, get the end of the right chord through the circle on the left side.
5. Next, pull both ends of the rope tightly. Try not to twist the cord.

With these steps, you have successfully made the first side of the square knot.

Now to complete the square knot, you have to do the same steps on the other side, so:

6. Set the external right cord over the other three, making a 4-shape.
7. Put the external left cord over the end of the right rope and under the two in the center.
8. As previously done, take the end of the left rope and get it through the circle on the right side.
9. Pull both ends of the rope tightly, trying not to wind it.

Numerous excellent macramé products are made basically by redoing a square knot usually in rows. Most crafters often substitute the square knot by leaving a gap which often brings out a remarkable look.

In the next pages, you can see the step-by-step pictures to create a Square Knot.

Tip :A spiral of square knots can be tied with a sinnet of square knot made in the same direction (repeat only step 1-5). If you alternate the directions without leaving space between knots, you will tie a flat braid (from 1 to 9 step, as instructed).

Alternating Square Knots Pattern

This is the perfect knot to use for hanging baskets, decorations, or any projects that are going to require you to put weight on it. Use a heavier weight cord for this, which you can find at craft stores or online. Do not rush and make sure you have even tension throughout.. Numerous excellent macramé products are made by repeating sets of square knots, usually in rows.

Most artisans often use alternate square knots, leaving free space between the rows. This pattern is highly appreciated, very simple to reproduce, and makes projects beautiful.

Here is the structure of the alternating square knot pattern:

1. Start with knitting four Lark's Head knots that produce eight strings.
2. Use the four strings on the left to make a square knot.
3. Next, make another square knot with the four cords on the right.
4. Finally, assembles another square knot with the four cords in the center (you can push away the others strings: this is the best approach to make it easier).
5. Repeat this model (left strings, right cords, central strings) until you wish. Make sure to tighten the ropes every time.

Some tips to remember:

- Leave heavenly gaps between each line, working your way down the entire thing.
- Knit your knot securely before starting to make the next one.
- Work on one side of the piece and then tie the knot on the other.
- Bring the knot to the center and ensure enough cords lengths on both sides.
- Pull the knot securely up to the center of the cord, then move on to the following cord.
- It is a matter of sequence. Work the one side, then go back to the beginning, work the center then go back to the other side once more.
- Continue to do this for as long as your cords are or as needed for the project.

Wrapping Knot

This knot is widely used as the start and end of macrame projects for tying a bunch of threads together.

1. Make a U-shape with one end of the cord. Next, hold the U-shaped cord against the filler cords with the short and long ends facing up and then the bent U-part facing down.

2. Begin wrapping around all of the cords (including the short end) with the long end of the wrapping cord. Proceed to wrap from up to bottom, and be sure to keep the wraps all snug together but not overlapping.

3. Once you've made all the wraps you need to make, loop the wrapping cord through the loop created by the bottom of the U-shape. Next, pull the top cord sticking out of the wraps, short end of the working cable, to tighten the loop.

4. Keep pulling the top cord until the loop draws up into the wraps about halfway. You don't want it to come up out of the top of the wraps.

5. Now you can trim the two ends of the wrapping cord and push the ends down into the wraps.

Josephine Knot

I love this knot because it looks like a jewel. It gives each macrame project an air of very special preciousness and delicacy. You can use it to create beautiful necklaces, belts and bracelets but also to decorate wall hangers and plant baskets.

Below is the guide to make the Josephine Knot:

1. Tie a Lark's Head Knot with two cords to have four cords to tie.
2. Take the left cords and loop them under themselves, forming a horizontal teardrop shape.
3. Take your right cords and place them over the loop of the left cords.
4. Put the right cords over the left cords that are coming from the knot up top, then bring the right cord under the length of the left cord,
5. Then the right cords go over themselves and then under the ends of the left cords. Basically, the right cords must go over and under, then again over and under from left to right.

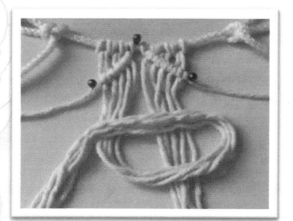
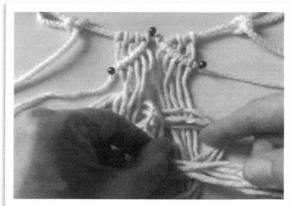

Leaf Pattern

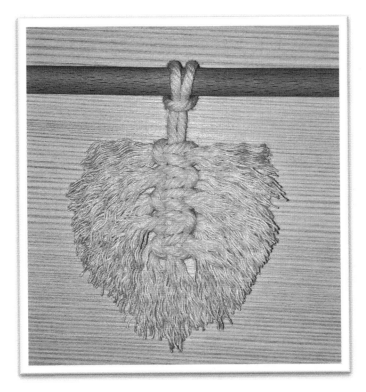

This simple yet beautiful pattern can be used to create all kinds of projects, from dream catchers to jewelry and plant hangers. It is also a great way to recycle all the excess pieces of rope that we find scattered around our work surface.

In the project the string pieces are all the same length, but they don't need to be, just tie the pairs of string from longest to shortest to the vertical string.

To execute it, follow the instruction and the pictures shown below:

Materials:

- 160 cm/48 inches (or 8 Pieces of 20 cm/5 inches) of Cord
- 1 Piece of 40 cm/10 inches of Cord
- A Dowel
- Scissors
- Measuring Tape

Instructions:

1. Take the cord 40 cm long, fold it in half, then tie it with a Lark's Head Knot to the dowel.

2. Cut 10 pieces of 20 cm/5 inches of cord, then take one of them, fold it in half, and put it under the first one horizontally.

3. Grab another cord, fold it in half, and put it on the second one fixed string; insert the ends of the strings through the loops formed by opposite ropes; then pull the ends tightly, as shown below.

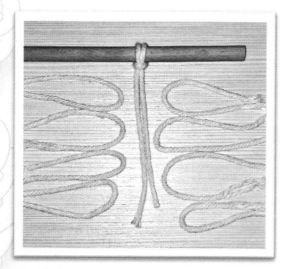

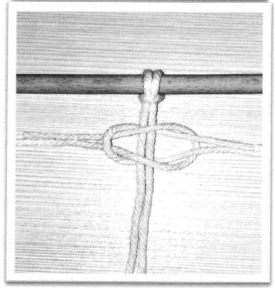

4. Repeat it once again. Fold another cord in half and put it under the fixed one on the opposite side, then take and fold another thread in half, insert the strings' ends through the loops formed by opposite ropes, then pull the ends tightly.

5. Set all the cords to the fixed one and complete the leaf.

6. Pull all the knots tightly.

7. Unfold, comb, and cut the extended cords in leaf shape.

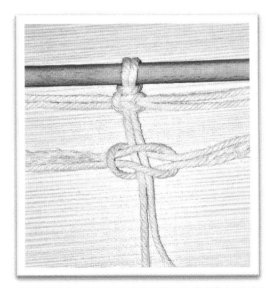 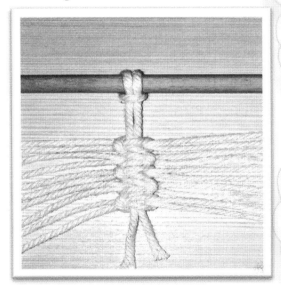

Diamond Squares Pattern

We continue to study fascinating macramé, presenting another pattern for beginners.

To execute it, follow the instruction below:

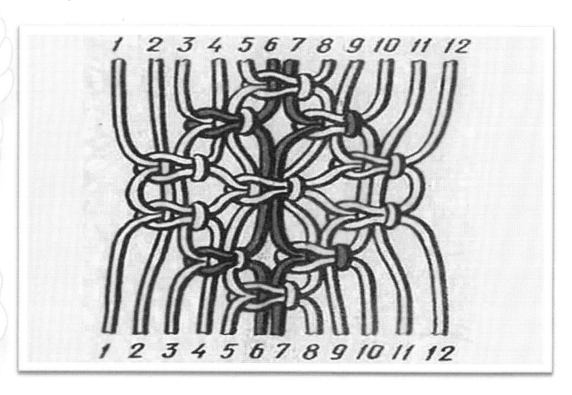

1. Fold each of the six threads in half and tie them in a row with six Lark's Head Knots. You will get a total of twelves strings. In the picture all threads are numbered.

2. Make the First row taking the center's cords (5, 6, 7, and 8) and tie a Square Knot.

3. Make the second row tying a square knot with the 3, 4, 5, 6 threads, and another with the 7, 8, 9, 10 cords.

4. Now tie the third row, making two square knots with the 1, 2, 3, 4 threads and 9, 10, 11, 12 cords.

5. Repeat the row 1.

6. Repeat the row 3.

7. Repeat the row 2.

8. Repeat the row 1.

Macramé Flower Pattern

Aren't flowers gorgeous? For them to attract your eyes, they don't always have to be real.

One of our best activities to do is making flowers to add to our macramé projects. It places a spotlight on what you have made. You will feel that it will enable your project alive by incorporating numerous types of flower styles and leaf/feather patterns.

We like to add to our wall hanging parts an array of assorted macramé flowers, and we also like to pair them with the other natural macramé-shaped designs, such as feathers or leaves.

We will not consider it to be incredibly challenging for this project. We will place this project between the level of intermediate and advanced skills. We faced this unique project because of the number of knots we had to create using such a thin string to shape the flower pattern. Although it is not a big concern, you will find that on a project like jewelry bracelets, necklace, and macramé flowers identical to this one using smaller diameter cord, you will be expected to spend as much time, if not more time, creating these smaller projects as compared to those of the medium or larger project by using thicker cord such as the macramé plant hanger or a wall hanging. However, learning how to make the macramé flower can dramatically boost your patience, your techniques of binding, and give you lots of practice to expand on your macramé basis.

To acquire a strong understanding of how to create this pattern, try to make these macramé flowers and give them a try.

Materials:

- Scissors
- Measuring Tape
- Crochet Needle (optional)
- 1 x 1mm hole beads
- 12 x 8-feet/250m cotton cord (3mm)

Instructions:

1. Take one of the pieces of cord fold it in half and secure it to your workspace.
2. Attach the rest of the cords to that main cord using vertical half hitch knots: Wrap the right side of the cord over and around and then pull it through. Repeat that process down below the first wrap and pull it through the hole: that's your first vertical half hitch knot.
3. Do that same thing again on the other side and be sure to pull it nice and tight, so that the knots line up right next to each other; slide those knots to the end and then attach the rest.
4. Tie a row of double half-hitch knots down the left side.
5. Do the same thing on the right side, and then when you get to the end time one more double half-hitch knot to attach the two sides.
6. Flip your work so the left side is facing down; find the 7th cord from the top and then do a row of double half-hitch knots in the opposite direction.
7. Do the same thing on the right side flip your work back up and down and then tie another row of regular double half-hitch knots going down the left side.

8. Repeat on the right side flip your work with the left side facing down again and then find the 8th cord from the top and do another row of double half-hitch knots in the opposite direction.

9. Repeat this on the right side now you're going to tie four regular rows of double half-hitch knots on both sides.

10. Flip your work with the left side facing down again and then find the ninth cord from the top and tie another row of double half-hitch knots in the opposite direction.

11. Repeat this on the right side as well now tie three more rows of regular double half-hitch knots on both sides for the last row.

12. After you tie a double half-hitch knot, you will hold the working cord with the filler cords and then tie the next knot around them to finish off the edge.

13. Repeat that processes on the right side and also repeat this entire process four more times.

14. Now attach these cords together with a wrapping knot: first take two strands of the string from each flower petal and hold it up so that we can use that later for fringe bundle the petals up and overlap them a little bit so they kind of look like a tropical flower.

15. Flip the flower over and hold them very tight at the base and then you're going to tie a wrapping knot right at the bottom to hold everything in place

16. Trim down the fringe in the middle I trim it pretty long here. I ended up trimming it down shorter later on flip the flower back over and then pull on all the strings by the base to get it nice and tight

17. Fluff up your fringe and trim it down if you need to and you're done!

Things to Remember

Finally, we are at the end of the theoretical part of the book. The next step is to move on to the practical part and explore how these principles can be applied in simple starter works.

But before starting to knot, we need to have a recap of what you have learned so far.

First, we discussed the fundamentals of knot tying - the various types of knots, how to make different types of loops, and how to tie them. To begin mastering macramé projects, there are four main knots to learn - Lark's head knot, Square knot, Half Hitch knot, and Gathering knot. Once you have perfected these essential macramé knots, you will be able to create an infinite number of combinations with just these few fundamental knots.

Additionally, it is essential to understand the different types of cords used for macramé projects. The most common type of cord used for macramé is 2mm-3mm cotton, but other materials such as leather and wool are also sometimes used. 4mm-10 mm cotton cords are also used for bigger projects such as wall hangings and hammocks.

The third essential skill to learn is how to tie, secure, and finish the knots in a macramé project. It requires basic knowledge of weaving techniques, such as ensuring the weaves are tight and even. Additionally, it's essential to ensure that the cords' ends are secured tightly and securely so that they won't unravel or come undone.

Then, we explored the different ways of combining knots in sequences to make even more complex designs; we also discussed various techniques that can be used to create interesting patterns in ropes and threads. An essential step in mastering macramé is learning the weaving patterns that can be used to form a variety of designs. The Alternating Half-Hitch technique and the Square Knot pattern are two common weaving patterns.

With the Alternating Half-Hitch technique, two sets of half-hitches are used to form a weave in a back-and-forth motion. The Square Knot pattern is created by knotting four cords together alternately. To create more complex designs, combinations of weaving techniques can be used.

Finally, once you have perfected the knots and weaving patterns, it is time to get creative with color. The range of colors available for your macramé project is wide, so have fun mixing and matching threads to create unique designs.

Once you have learned these basics, it will be much easier to create beautiful macramé projects. With practice and persistence, you can learn how to create intricate patterns using a combination of knots and different types of cords.

Macramé projects can range from small wall hangings to larger pieces such as hammocks and furniture. With the right supplies, a little bit of practice, and some patience, you will be able to master these beautiful macramé knots and create stunning art pieces with just some basic skills.

In the following chapters, you will discover some beginner's project ideas to start your macramé journey. I hope you will find them helpful and have fun.

Dear Reader,

Thank you for taking the time to read my book.

Writing and publishing a book is no small feat – it takes hard work and dedication to create something that offers value to readers like you, and I'm so grateful that you took the time to experience what I had to offer.

I hope that you enjoyed the fruits of my hard work and found the content engaging and thought-provoking.

If you liked what you read, please leave an honest review on Amazon. Your feedback is invaluable in helping other readers discover and enjoy my book.

Thanks again for taking the time to read it and for considering leaving a review.

Macramé Jewelry Projects

Macrame Earrings

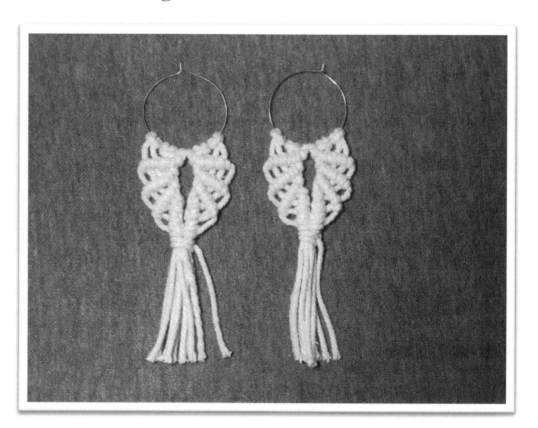

Materials:

- 10 meters/33 feet of cord (or 20 pieces of 50 cm/20 inches of cord)
- Scissors
- Ruler
- T pins or tape ruler
- 2 Pieces of ear-ring

Bunches utilized: Lark's Head Knot, Half Hitch Knot and Diagonal Double Hitch Knot.

Instructions:

1. Cut ten pieces of 50cm/20 inches of cord and tie them on an ear-ring with Lark's Head Knots. You can pin the ring or fix it with a tape ruler to make it fix on your project table.

2. Weave a row of Diagonal Double Half Hitch knots on the left, using as working cord the #5 as previous shown.

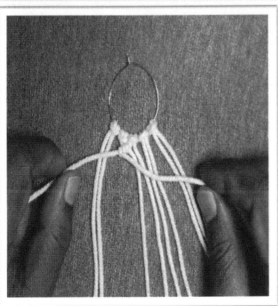
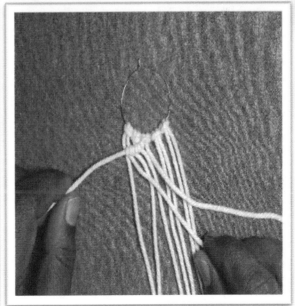

3. Weave a row of Diagonal Double Half Hitch knots on the right, using as working cord the #6 as shown below.

4. Tie another two rows of Diagonal Double Half Hitch knots on both side of the work as shown below..

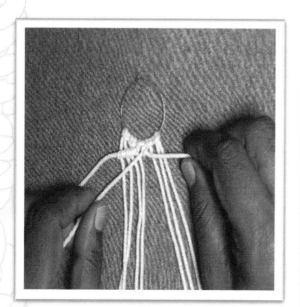
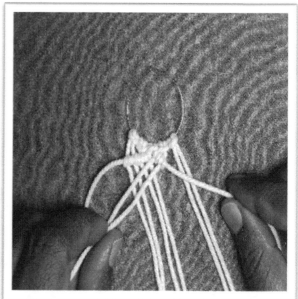

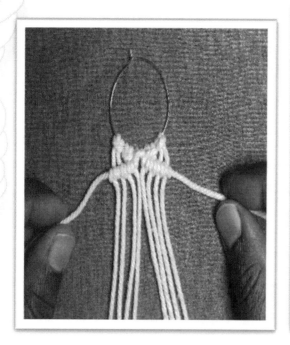
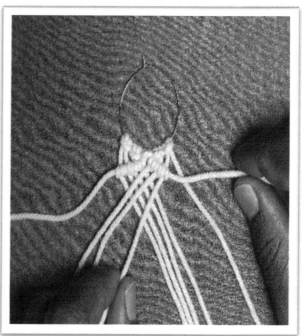

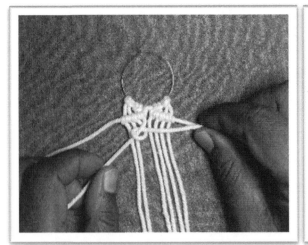
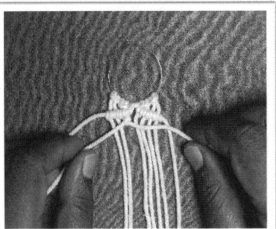

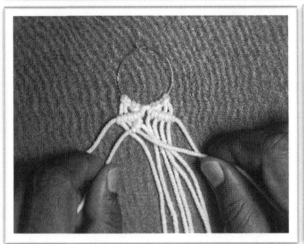
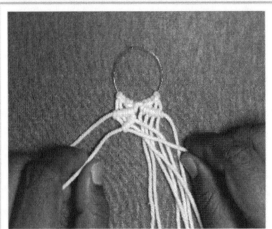

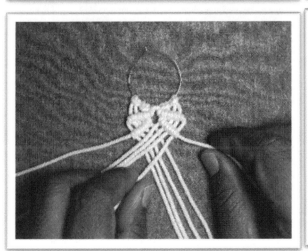
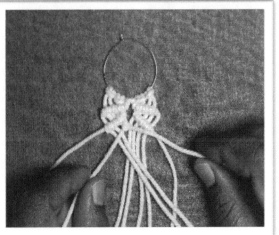

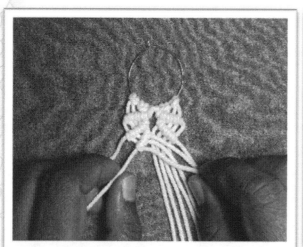

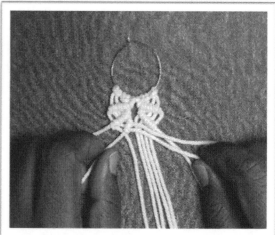

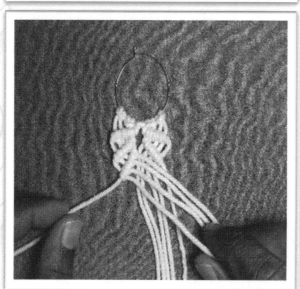

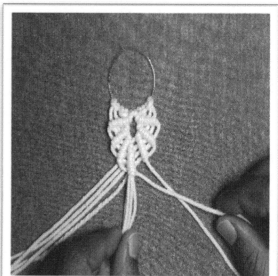

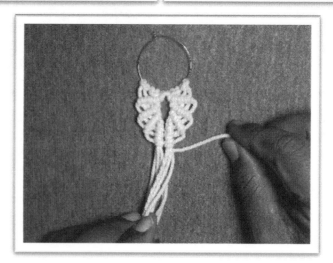

5. Connect the both side with three half hitch knots, leave 5 cm/2 inches of cords free and cut the rest.

6. Make the same steps for the other ear ring.

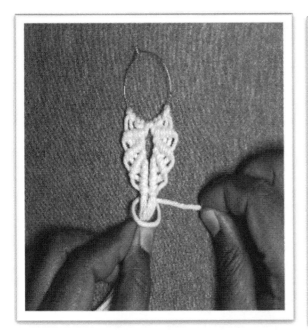
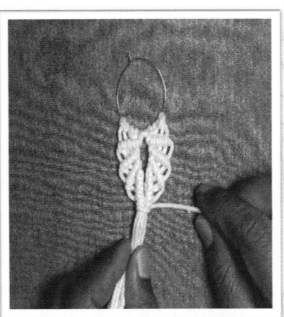

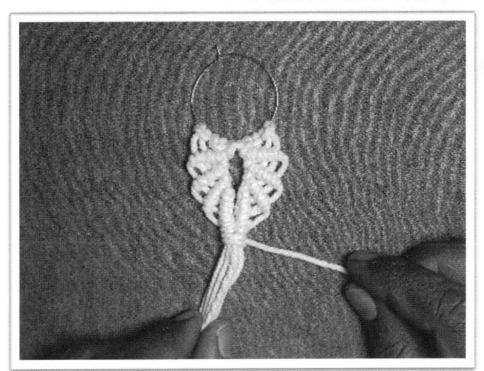

Macrame Necklace

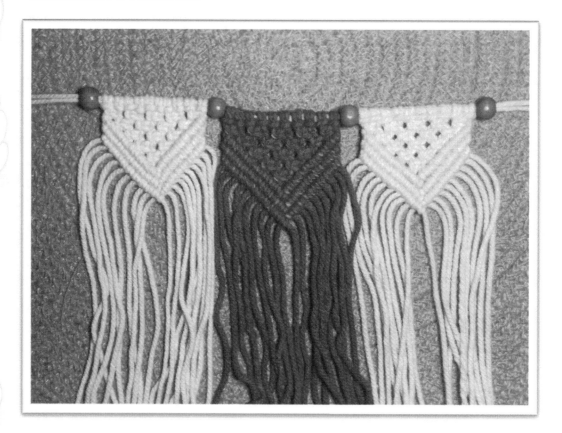

Materials:

- 10 meters/33 feet of red color cord (or 10 pieces of 100 cm red color cords /40 inches of red cord)
- 20 meters/66 feet of white color cord (or 20 pieces of 100 cm/40 inches white color cord).
- 1 Pieces of 150 cm/60 inches white cord.
- Scissors
- Ruler
- T pins or tape ruler
- 4 Pieces of crystal or wooden beads.

Bunches utilized: Lark's Head Knot, Square Knot and Diagonal Double Hitch Knot.

Instructions:

1. Take 150cm cord and fold it half, then add 10 Pieces of 100cm/40 inches of red cord with Lark's Head Knot.

2. Tie a row of five Square Knots.

3. Again, leave two cords from the both side of the work and wave a row of four-square knots.

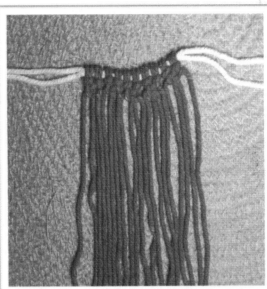

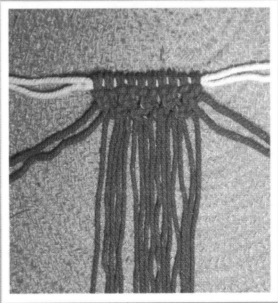

4. Leave two cord s from the both side of the work and tie a row of four-Square knots.

5. Again, leave two cords from the both side of the work and wave a row of four-square knots

6. Continue to tie the last three rows of square knots: leave two cords from the both side of the work and wave three square knots, then two square knots and only one in the last row. The entire sequence is showed below.

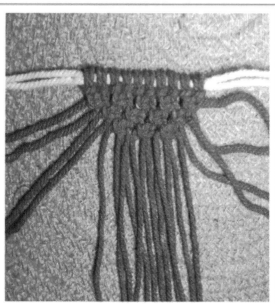
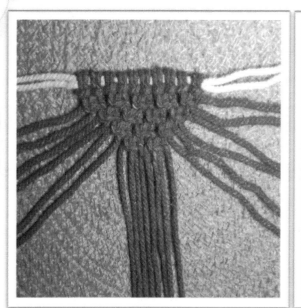
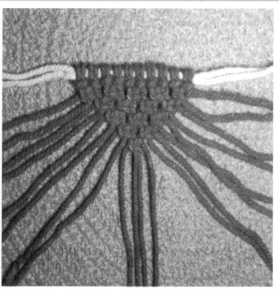

7. Weave three layers of five Double Half Hitch Knots for both side of the work, one side at time, as showed below. At the end, horizontally cut the rest of the strings to the length you like best.

8. Add one wooden bead on both side of the white cord. The first part of the work is completed. You can choose to wear the necklace just like this or make the other two white triangles just repeating the previous steps, like I did. In the next two pages is showed all the process.

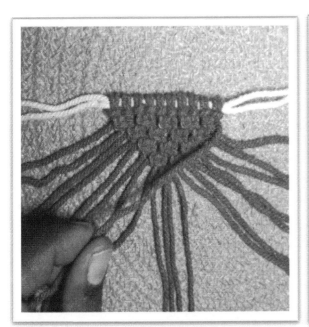
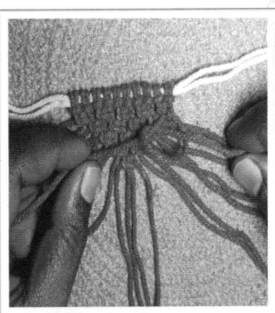
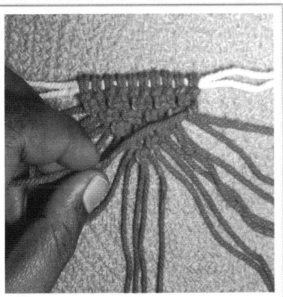
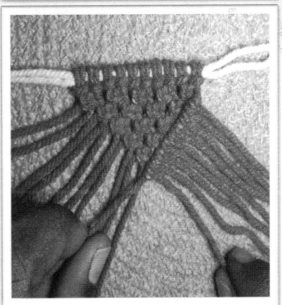

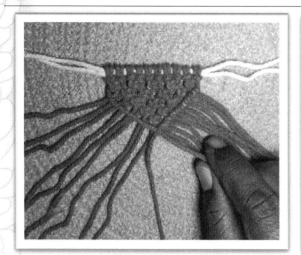
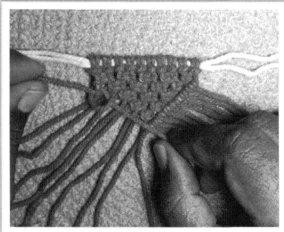

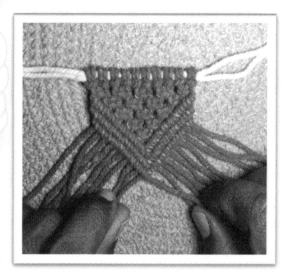
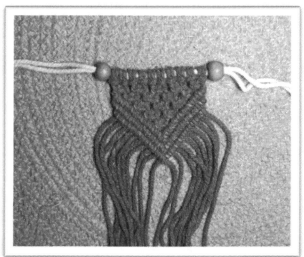

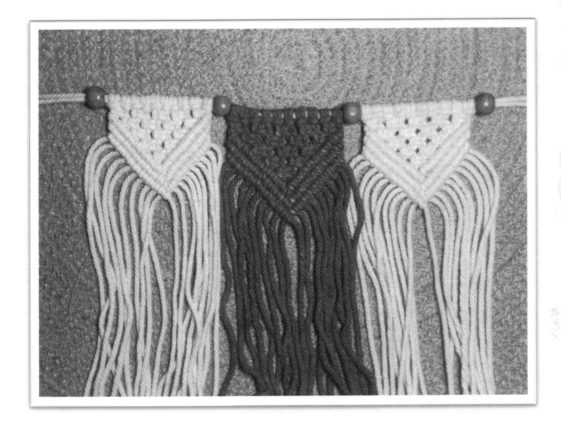

Macrame Wrist Lace

Materials:

- 6 meters/240 inches of red color cord (or 6 pieces of 100 cm red color cords /40 inches of red cord)
- 6 meters /240 inches of white color cord (or 6 pieces of 100 cm/40 inches white color cord).
- 24 Pieces of multi color beads.
- Scissors
- Ruler
- T pins or tape ruler

Bunches utilized: Alternating Square Knots.

Instructions:

1. Divide the pieces of string into three clusters of four cords each: the first group must have all red strings, the second two red strings, and two white strings; the third group only white cords.

2. Tape the top ends with a tape ruler to your work surface, leaving 4cm free, and tie a square knot for each batch of cords.

3. Secure the three-Square Knots close to each other with T-pins, with the bicolor group in the center, as showed below. They will be your first row.

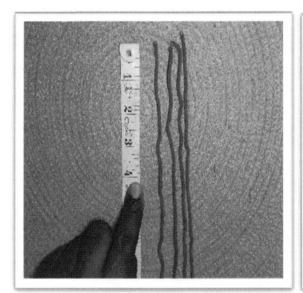
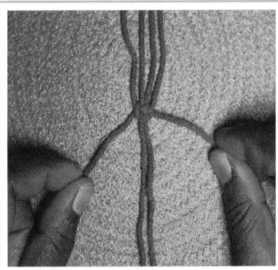
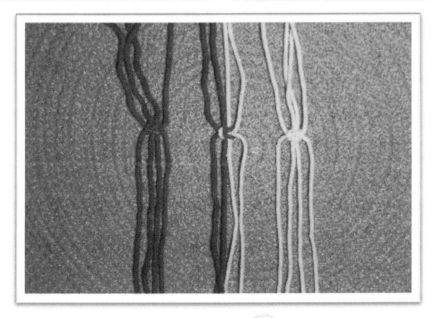

4. Tie a square knot to the left to join the first and second cluster of ropes, putting the first two cords to the left of the first cluster aside.

5. Make the same things to the other half side of the work: wave a square knot to join the second and third group of cords, putting the last two cords to the right of the third cluster aside, as showed below. Now you have done the second row of your work.

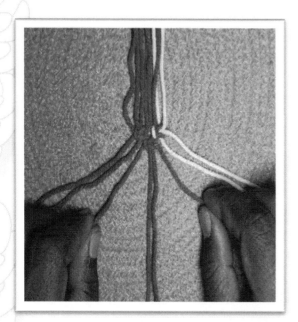

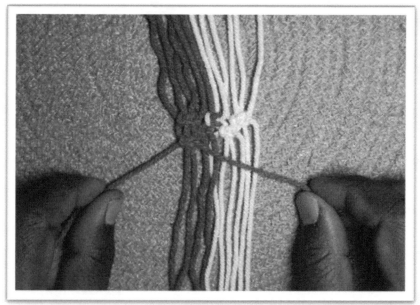

6. To tie the third row, make right under the second row a Square knot with the firsts four red cords, then continue to knot the two square knots from the left to the right side.

7. Repeat the step 5-6 and keep making rows of knots until you reach the diameter of your wrist.

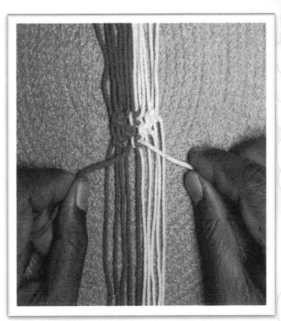

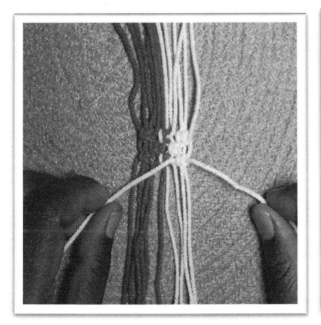
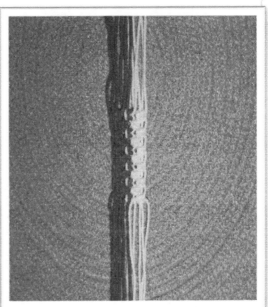

8. Add a bead to the end of each string and tie the end with an overhand knot.

9. Finally, put the bracelet on your wrist and tie it with a large overhand knot to secure it.

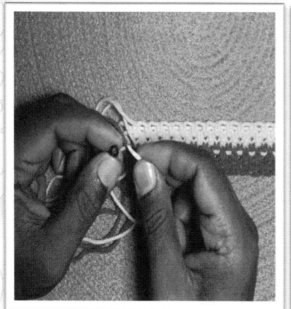
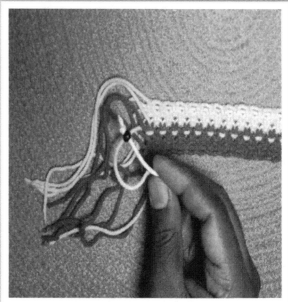

Home Décor Macramé Projects

Macrame Coaster of the Heart

Materials:

- 16 meters/53 feet of cord (or 32 Pieces 50 cm/20 inches of cord).
- Scissors
- Ruler
- T pins or tape ruler

Bunches utilized: Square Knots.

Instructions:

1. Get 4 Pieces of 50 cm/20 inches cord, leave 5cm/2 inches from the top and make a square knot

2. Apply square knots to another 12-piece 50cm/20 inches cords. Now you will have 4 separated square knots. You can pin them or fix with the ends with a tape ruler to make them fix on your project table.

3. Join the firsts two square knotted groups of cords by applying another square knot: leave free the two cords on the left and the lasts on the right.

4. Repeat the step 3 again with the other two groups of cords.

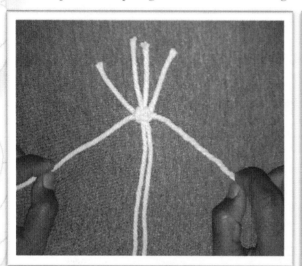
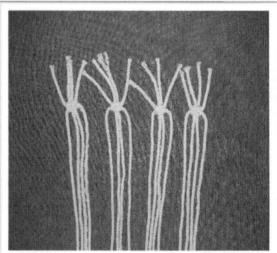
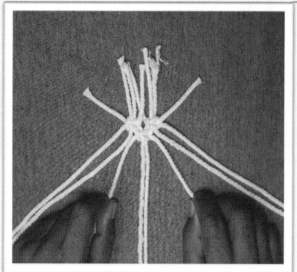
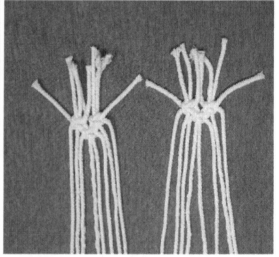

 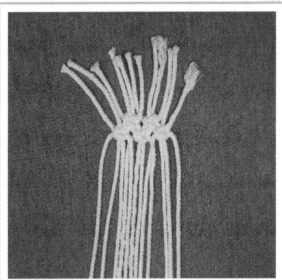

5. Add two cords from the left side and apply square knot.

6. Add two cords from the right side apply square knot.

7. Again insert two cords from the left and right side and weave square knot.

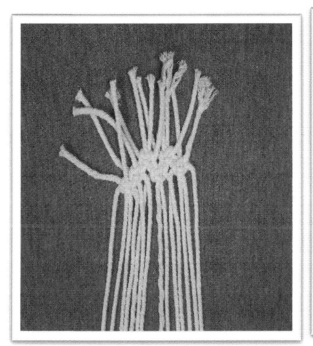 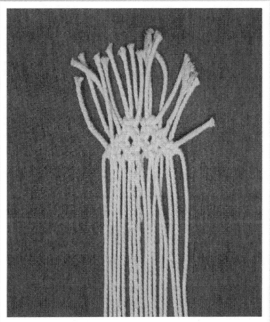

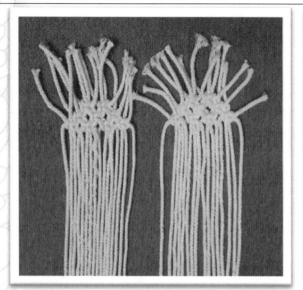 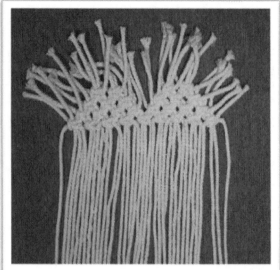

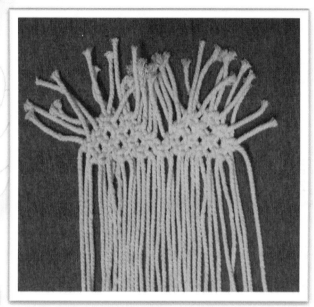 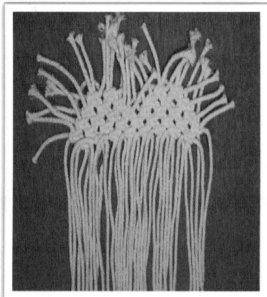

8. Repeat the same process with the other group of cords.

9. Join them together with a row of square knot.

10. Add 2 cords from the right side apply square knot, leave two cords from the both side and make another row of square knots on both sides. Again leave two cords from the both side and tie a row of square knots. Continue the same process until you will tie a row with an only one square knot. In the next page the steps of the process.

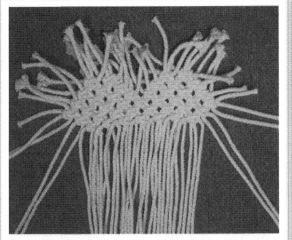

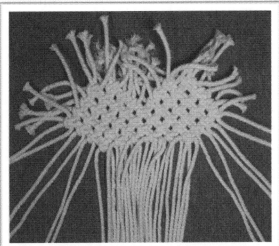

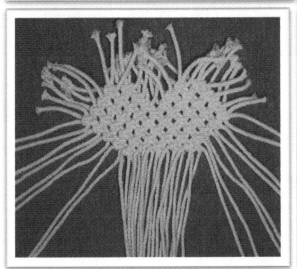

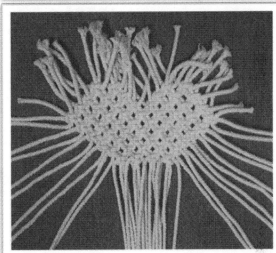

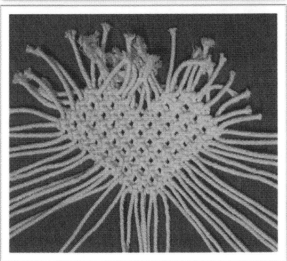

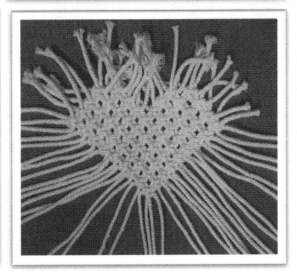

11. Cut the ends of the cord at the same length with sharp scissors , unfold them and comb them with a hair comb to make them fluffy.

Macramé Journal Mark

Materials:

- 720 cm/300 inches of cord (+ one little piece of 20 cm/10 inches)
- Scissors
- Ruler
- Wooden bead

Bunches utilized: Lark's Head Knot and Diagonal Hitch knot.

Instructions:

1. Cut 4 pieces of cord of 180 cm (72 inches) (each and another one piece of cord of (10 inches) 20 cm.
2. Secure the smaller cord to a desk with a tape.
3. Fold in half the 4 piece of cord and attach them to the smaller piece with a Lark's head knot.
4. Tie seven diagonal hitch knots from the left to the right to create the first row.
5. Repeat in the same direction until you will tie 14 or 15 rows.
6. Cut the ends of cords at the desired length, unravel and comb them to make a fringe
7. Detach the work from the desk, insert the wooden bead through the ends of the smaller cord and tie them with a simple knot to close the project.

I recommend to use a small sized cord (1-3 mm). It could seem difficult to manage cords so small, but the pattern is simple and will be a good starting project. I love the soft feeling of natural cotton fiber for this type of work, but even a synthetic cord should be fine if you prefer a strength and resistant effect.

Macrame Round Coaster

Materials:

- 1 Piece of 200 cm/80 inches of cord
- 2 Pieces of 90 cm/36 inches of cord.
- 4 Pieces of 110 cm/44 inches of cord.
- 4 Pieces of 130 cm/52 inches of cord.
- 6 Pieces of 40 cm/16 inches of cord.
- Scissors
- Ruler
- T pins or tape ruler

Bunches utilized: Reverse Lark's Head Knot and Double Half Hitch Knot.

Instructions:

1. Take the 200 cm /80 inches cord and fix one of its ends to your working area with one or two T-pins.

2. Fold the three pieces of 130 cm/52 inches of cords in half and tie them to the fixed cord with three Reverse Lark's Head Knots near the end pinned. Next, pull the longer end of the longest rope to tighten the loop and make the work rounded, as shown below. Then start to tie the coaster using the longest end as the holding cord.

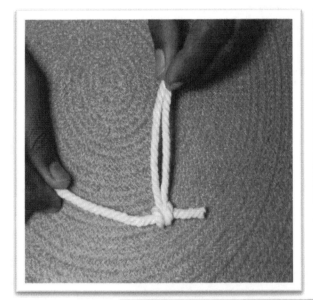
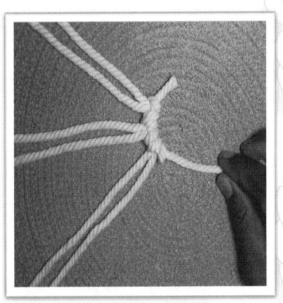

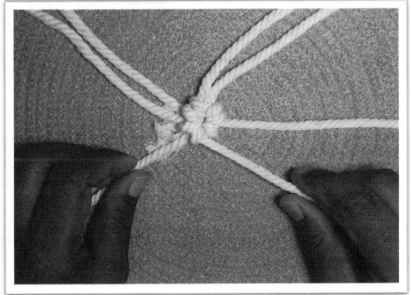

3. Tie the cords already attached with Double Half Hitch Knots on the holding rope.

4. Add the last 130 cm pieces of cord with a Reverse Lark's Head Knot to the holding cord.

5. Continue to tie Double Half Hitch Knots with the other cords, as shown.

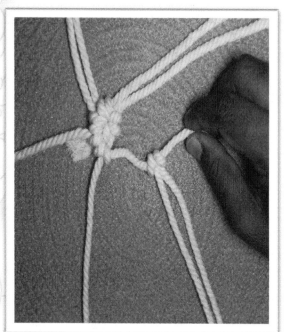
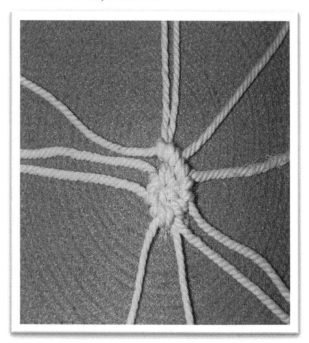

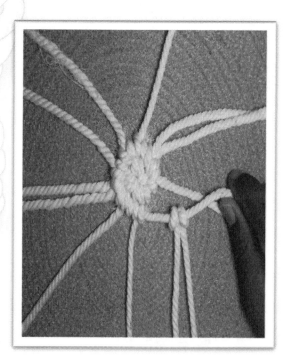
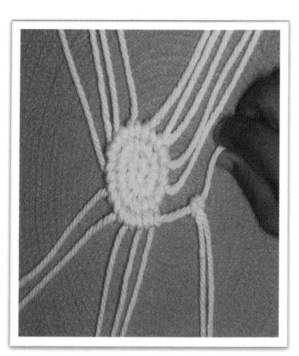

6. Going around the project, every time you notice a gap between the cords to tie, add a piece of the other threads remaining, from the longest to the smallest until all the cords will include and the final project gets to 12 cm diameter.

7. Finally, put the end of the holding cord into the back of the project, and unfold, comb, and cut the extended cords.

Macramé Wall Art

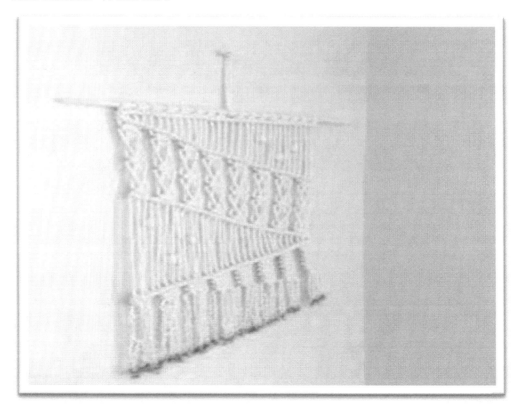

Adding a bit of Macramé to your walls is always fun because it livens up space without making it cramped—or too overwhelming for your taste. Plus, it looks beautiful without being too complicated to make. You can check it out below!

Materials:

- Large wooden beads
- Acrylic paint
- Painter's tape
- Paintbrush
- Wooden dowel
- 70 yards/64 meters rope

Bunches utilized: Lark's Head Knot, Diagonal Double Hitch Knot and switch knot.

Instructions:

1. Attach the dowel to a wall. It is best to just use removable hooks, so you will not have to drill anymore.

2. Cut the rope into 14 x 4 yard/3,6 meters pieces, as well as 2 x 5 yard/4,6 meters pieces. Use 5 yard/4,6 meters pieces to end the dowel with. Continue doing this with the rest of the rope.

3. Then, start making Lark's head knot to tie all the cords and continue all the way through, like what is shown below.

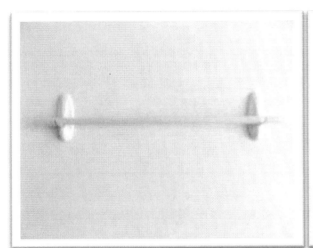 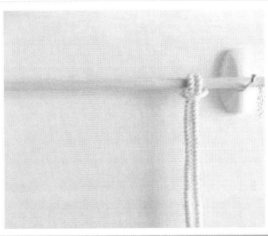

 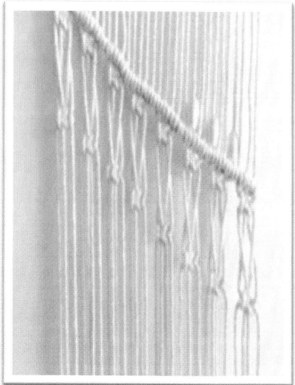

4. Once you get to the end of the dowel, start

   to tie double half hitch knots diagonally from the left to the right side. You can also add the wooden beads any way you want, so you would get the kind of décor that you need. Make sure to tie the knots after doing so.

5. Use four ropes to make switch knots[1] and keep the décor more secure. Tie around eight of these.

6. Add a double-half hitch and then tie them diagonally once again, from the right to the left side.

---

[1] switch knot is made by making a square knot then switching your filler cords and working cords so that in the next square knot, the filler cords will be your working cords and the working cords will be the filler cords. Then, make another square knot.

7. Add more beads and then trim the ends of the rope.

8. Once you have trimmed the rope, go ahead, and add some paint to it. Summery or neon colors would be good.

 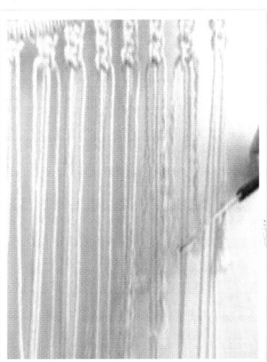

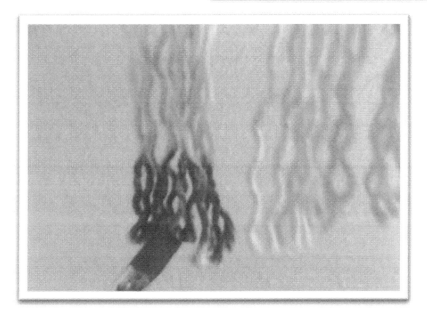

9.   That is, it! You now have your own Macramé Wall Art!

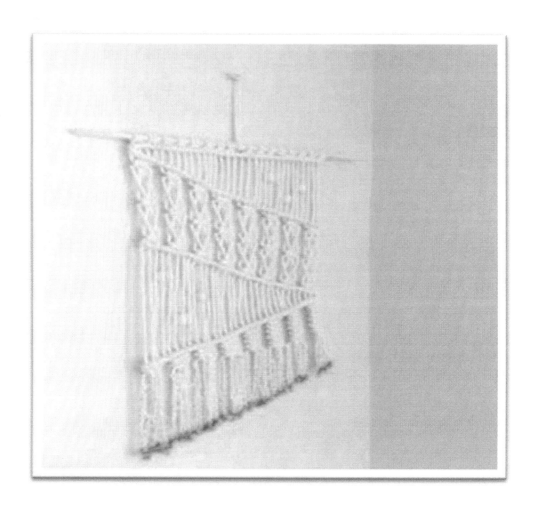

Macramé Book or Magazine Holder

Are you the kind of person who loves to get lost in a good book? For you, this macramé book holder project could be the ideal DIY macramé project if you love reading like us.

We made that project because we decided to add some kind of exclusive home décor to our bathroom; we wanted to hang up something beautifully pleasing and gave the character of the space and a little bit of our touch.

For this initiative, plan to set aside roughly 2–3 hours from start to finish.

Materials:

- 2 Wooden Dowel
- 24 Pieces of 120 inches/300 cm strands of cord

Bunches utilized: Lark's Head Knot, Square Knot

Instructions:

1. Start this project by binding a wooden dowel with Lark's Head knots.
2. Then tie twenty rows of alternating square knot.
3. Roll up the bottom portion of the pattern with the sides fastened together, making a wide enough pocket to accommodate the few magazines/couple of books.

Macrame Dreamcatcher

Materials:

- 1 Piece of 160 cm/63 inches of cord.
- 10 Pieces of 150 cm/60 inches of cord.
- 1 Piece of plastic or wood ring of 20 cm/7.87 inches
- Scissors
- Ruler
- T pins or tape ruler

Bunches utilized: Lark's Head Knot and Double Half Hitch Knot.

Instructions:

1. Tie a Lark's Head Knot to bind the first piece of 160 cm/63 inches of cord to the ring and, as shown.

2. Leave about 4 cm/1.5 inches on both sides of the first knot, then wave ten Lark's Head Knots, five per side, with the other 150 cm/60 inches of cord.

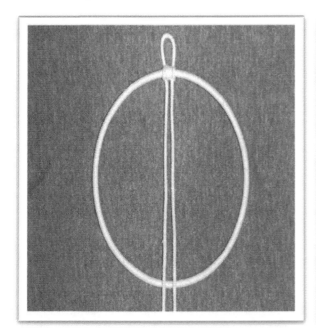

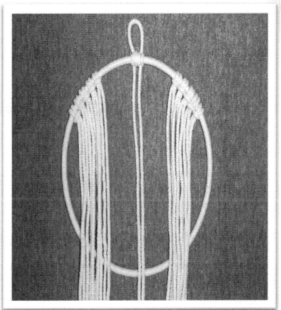

3. Tie a square knot about the 5 cm/2 inches position of the middle cords.

4. Wave another Square knot with the middle cords and the two cords adjacent on the left and right sides, as shown.

5. Again, make a square knot with the middle cords and the following two cords adjacent on both sides of the work.

6. Repeat steps 4-5 until all the cords are waved, as shown below.

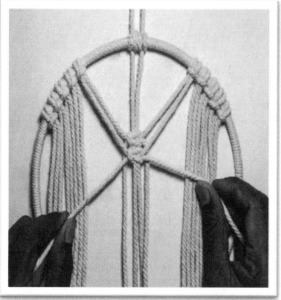
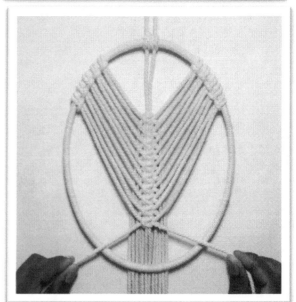

7. Now tie a Double Half Hitch Knot with the middle cords all around the ring..

8. Continue tying Double Hitch Knots with all the remaining cords on both sides of the work, as shown below.

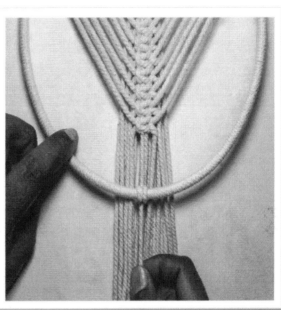

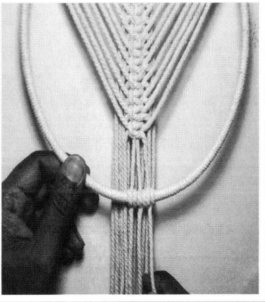

9. Cut the ends of the cords with sharp scissors at the length you prefer, unfold and comb them with a hair comb to make them fluffy.

*Variation: If you want to add movement, you can pick four cords on both sides of the work and the four central cords and wave a bunch of half-square knots in the same direction to create a spiral pattern. Finally, cut their ends at the same length, unfold and comb them.

Macramé Mini Wall Hanging

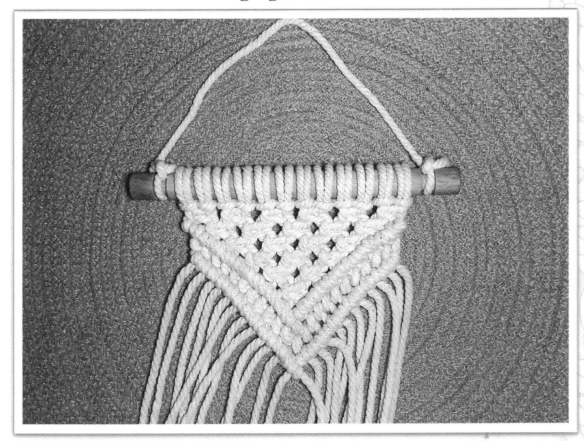

Materials:

- 10 meters/33 feet of cord (or 10 pieces of 100 cm /40 inches)
- 1 Pieces of 150 cm/60 inches white cord.
- A Wood Dowel
- Scissors
- Ruler
- T pins or tape ruler

Bunches utilized: Lark's Head Knot, Square Knot and Diagonal Double Hitch Knot.

Instructions:

1. Tie the twelve cords with lark's head knots on the wooden dowel.

2. Starting from the left, make six square knots to complete the first row.

3. For the second row, skip two cords on both sides of the work and wave five square knots.

4. Again, omit the first two cords and create four square knots to complete the third row.

5. Continue to tie the last three rows of square knots: leave two cords from both sides of the work and wave three square knots, then two square knots and only one in the last row. The entire sequence is shown above.

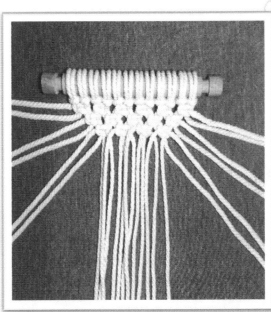

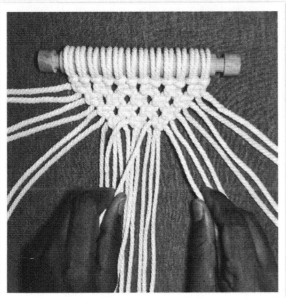
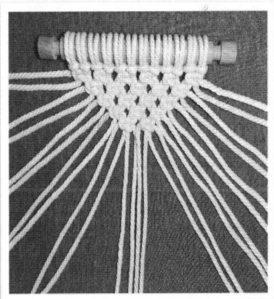

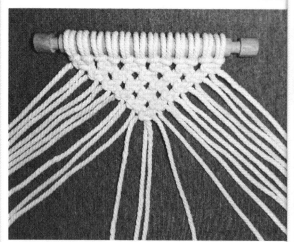
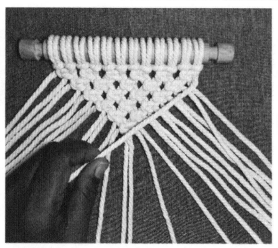
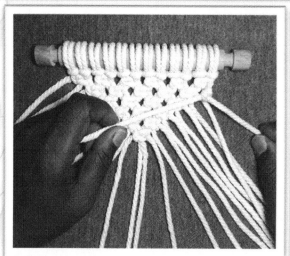

6. Turn backward the work, and using the first cord on the left as the holding cord, make ten double hitch knots towards the center.

7. Repeat this on the other side and join the two sides together with one double hitch knot towards the left.

8. Turn frontward and make another row of ten double hitch knots on both sides, as shown before.

9. Cut the cord in the shape of the design and comb out the ends.

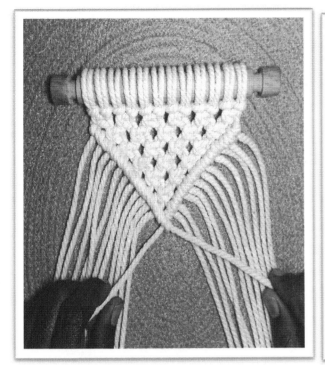
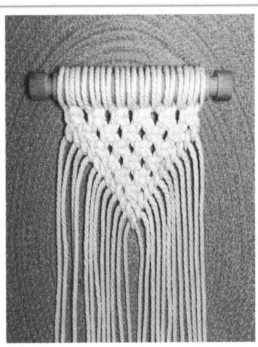

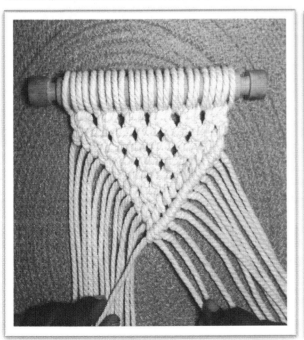
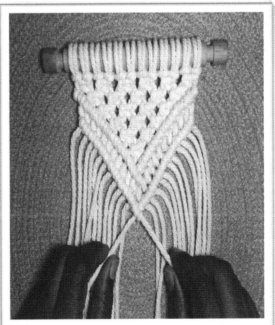

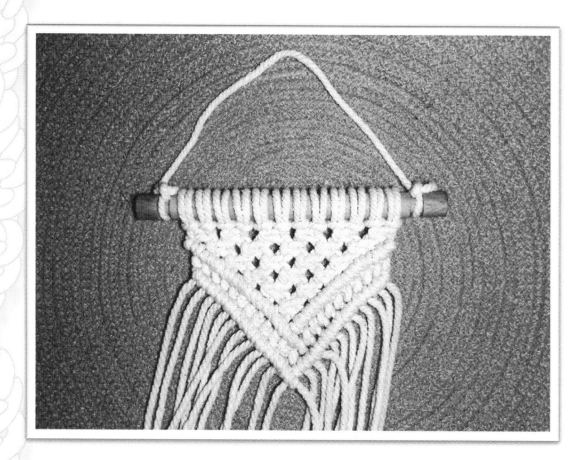

*Variation: If you want to add movement, leave 4 cm /1,5 inches of remaining cords free, pick two threads on both sides of the work and the two central threads, and wave a leaf pattern. Each leaf needs 16 pieces of 12 cm/5 inches cords. Cut every remaining cord and tie the threads without the leaves with simple overhand knots.

Macramé Hanging Garden Indoor and Outdoor Projects

Plant Hanger Bella

Materials:

- 8 Pieces of 140 inches/350 cm cord.
- 2 Pieces of 40 inches/100 cm cord.
- 16 Pieces of wooden beads.
- An S-Hook
- Scissors
- Ruler
- T pins or tape ruler

Bunches used: Half Knot, Lark´s Head Knot, Alternating Square Knot and Gathering Knot.

Instructions:

1. Take the eight pieces of 350 cm cord, align their ends, and divide them in half.

2. Measure 5cm before half of the bunch of cords and wrap the other 100cm piece of string around it for about 10cm so you can hang it; then fold the string group into a loop and tie it closed with a short gathering knot.

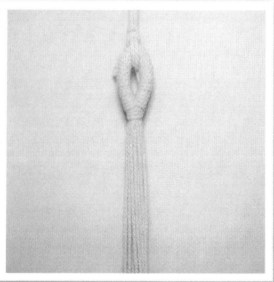

3. Divide the cords into four groups.

4. Take two pieces of rope from the first group and wave twenty half-knots.

5. Add a bead into the two middle cords.

6. Start to tie ten square knots on the same four cords.

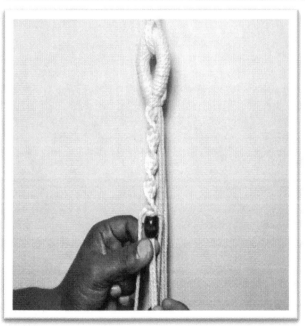
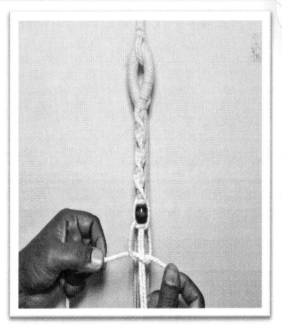

7. Insert another bead into the two middle cords and apply the other twenty half-knots with the same four cords.

8. Add a bead and tie ten square knots on the same four cords.

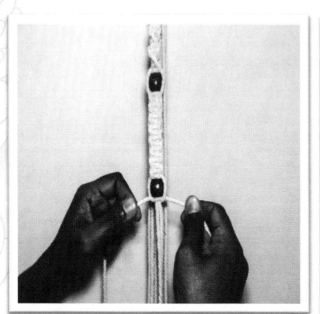
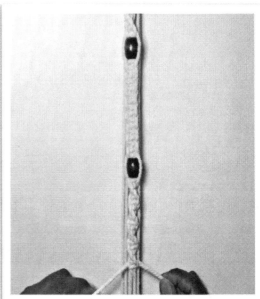
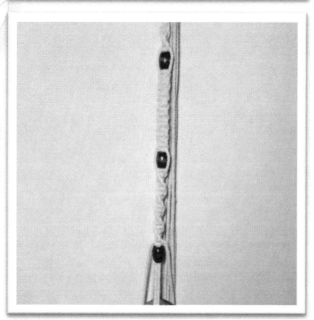
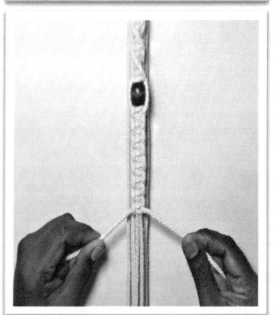

9. Repeat the 4-8 steps to the other three groups' cords.

10. Leave 8 cm, and weave one square knot between the adjacent square knots in all cords.

11. Again, leave 8 cm and weave another square knot between the adjacent square knots in all cords.

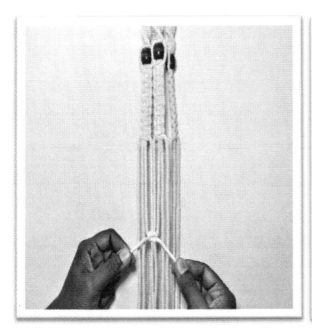
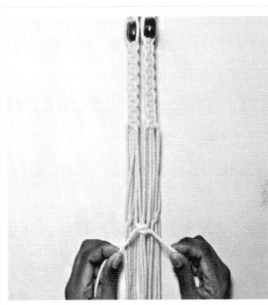
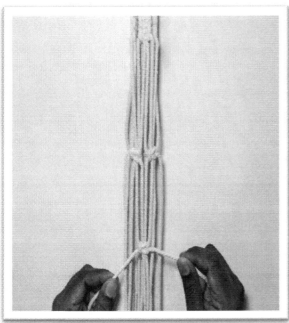
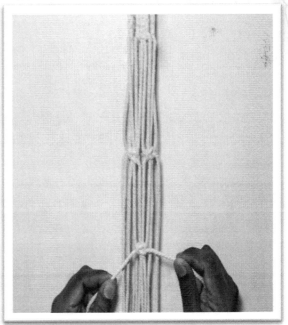

12. Leave free about 8cm and make a gathering wrap to close the bottom of the plant hanger with the other piece of 100cm cord, as illustrated in the pictures.

13. Cut the extended cord.

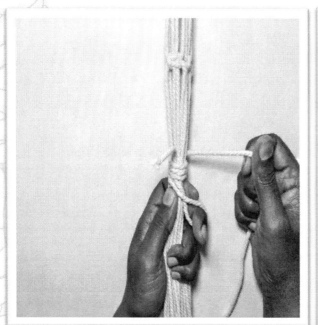
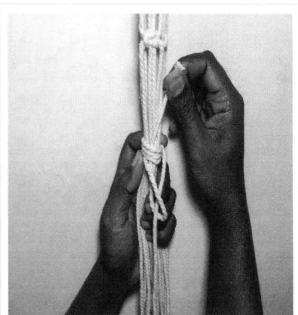
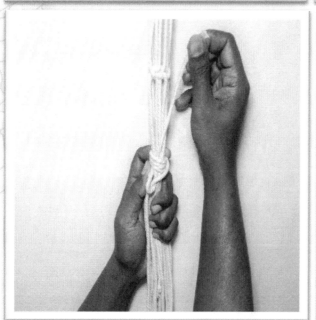

Macramé Plant Hanger Kathy

Materials:

- 4 Pieces of 140 inches/350 cm white cord.
- 4 Pieces of 140 inches/350 cm colored or white cord.
- 2 Pieces of 40 inches/100 cm cord.
- An S-Hook
- Scissors
- Ruler
- T pins or tape ruler

Bunches used: Half Knot, Lark´s Head Knot, Alternating Square Knot and Gathering Knot.

Instructions:

1. Take the eight pieces of 350 cm cord, align their ends, and divide them in half.

2. Measure 5cm before half of the bunch of cords and wrap the other 40 inches/100 cm piece of string around it for about 4 inches/10cm so you can hang it; then fold the string group into a loop and tie it closed with a short gathering knot.

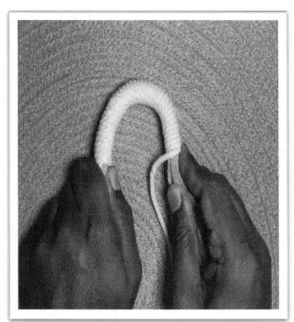

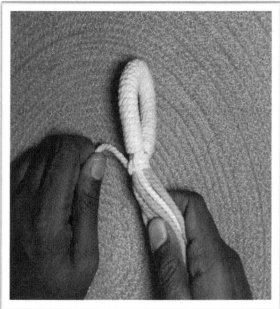

3. Divide the cords into four groups: if you use two cord colors, divide them in bunches of the same color.

4. Take four pieces of rope from the first group and wave thirty square knots.

5. Repeat for the other three groups' cords.

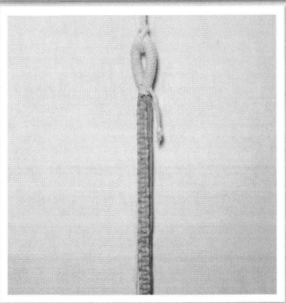
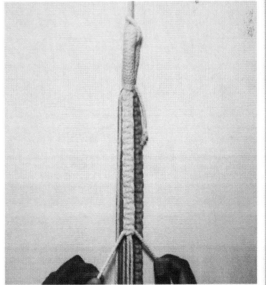

6. Leave 4 inches/10cm and weave four square knots between the adjacent cords, all around.

7. Again, leave 4 inches/10cm and make four square knots between the adjacent cords.

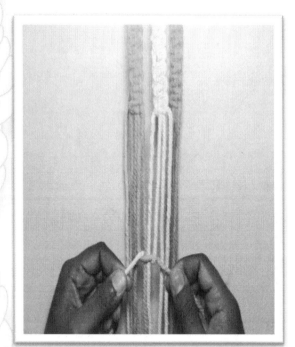
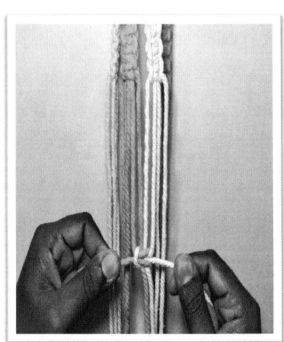
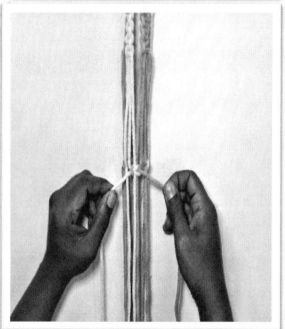
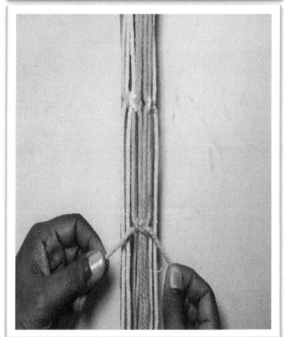

8. Live about 4 inches/10 cm apart, weave the gathering wrap with the other 40 inches/100cm of cord as demonstrated before, and cut the excess of cord.

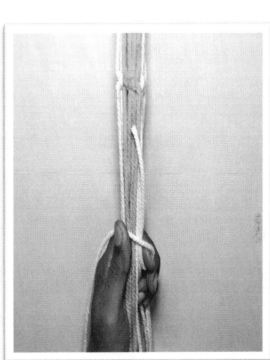
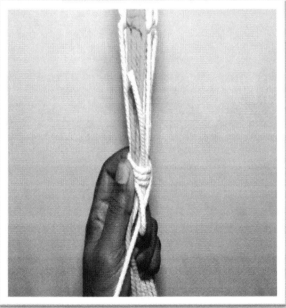

Macramé Plant Hanger Sarah

Materials:

- 6 Pieces of 100 inches/250 cm white cord.
- 4 Pieces of 100 inches/250 cm colored or white cord.
- An S-Hook
- 12 Pieces of wooden beads
- Scissors
- Ruler
- T pins or tape ruler

Bunches used: Square Knot, Alternating Square Knot and Gathering Knot.

Instructions:

1. Take eight pieces of 100 inches/250 cm of cord (four colored and four white), align their ends, and divide them in half.

2. Measure 5cm before half of the bunch of cords and wrap the other 40 inches/100 cm piece of string around it for about 4 inches/10cm so you can hang it; then fold the string group into a loop and tie it closed with a short gathering knot.

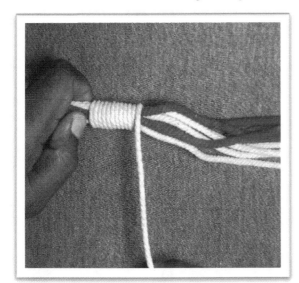
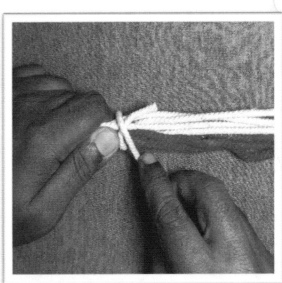

3. Divide the cords into four groups: if you use two cord colors, divide them in bunches of the same color.

4. Take four pieces of rope from the first group and wave three square knots.

5. Leave 2 inches/5 cm of cord and make eight square knots.

6. Leave again 2 inches/5 cm of cord and make three square knots, then add three wooden bead into the two bunch central cords.

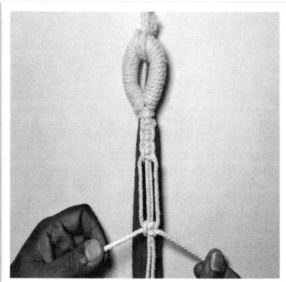
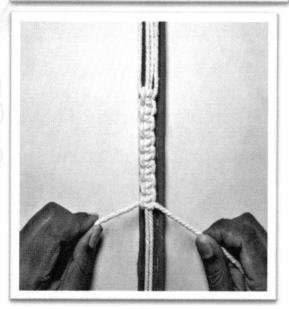
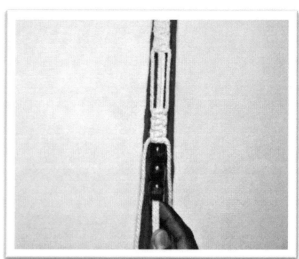

7. Tie three square knots.

8. Repeat the steps 4-7 for the rest of the cord bunches.

9. Leave 4 inches/10cm and weave four square knots between the adjacent cords, all around.

10. Again, leave 4 inches/10cm and make four square knots between the adjacent cords.

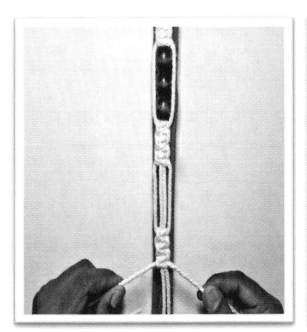

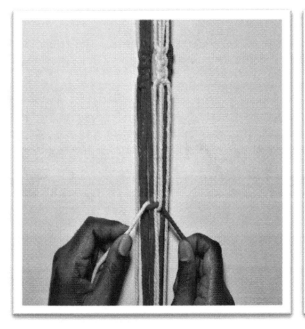
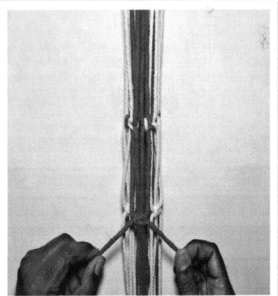

11. Live about 4 inches/10 cm apart, weave the gathering wrap with the other 40 inches/100cm of cord as demonstrated below, and cut the excess of cord.

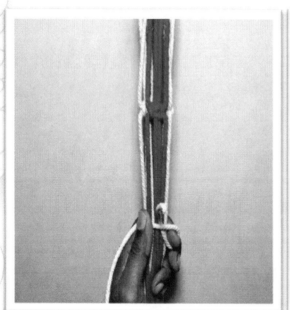
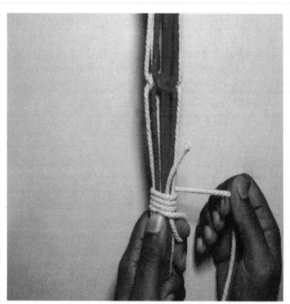

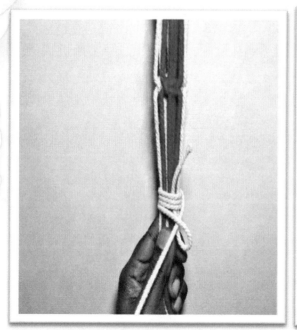
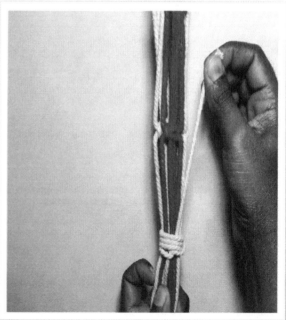

The Comeback of Macramé and How You Can Profit

Selling Your Creations

Macramè is a timeless craft that can be aesthetically pleasing and highly lucrative. So if you have an eye for design, macramé might be the perfect way to make some extra money on the side, or even as a full-time job.

Thanks to the internet, making money with macramé is easier than ever. With online marketplaces like Etsy and other online communities, macramé artists can reach a broad audience and make a living from their art. Best of all, the demand for quality macramé keeps growing.

There are several ways you can sell your creations:

- Set up an Etsy shop and start selling your handmade goods immediately

- Start a blog focused solely on your macramé business — add patterns, and tutorials, sell e-books and finished pieces

- Showcase your work at craft fairs or art galleries in your local area

- Set up your website through which to sell and promote your items

To get started with selling macramé, there are a few critical steps you need to take. First, decide which product you want to make and sell. Popular items include wall hangings, plant hangers, purses, rugs, jewelry, and more. Each item will require different materials and techniques so be sure to research the best options for your product. Then, decide on the process you will use to make the items - hand knotting, crocheting or even utilizing a loom if you are ambitious.

Promote yourself online and offline — post pictures of what you're making on social media, and ask friends and family to spread the word about your store or blog.

As a macramé artist, it is important to stay up-to-date with the latest trends to meet the demands of your customers. Follow other macramé artists on social media, join relevant online communities and take advantage of any workshops or classes available in your area.

Next, create an online shop and list your products. Take quality photos that show off your creations and be sure to describe them accurately with compelling copy. Once your shop is looking good, promote it through various channels such as social media and forums. With a bit of effort, you'll soon find buyers for your gorgeous Macrame creations.

Remember to set fair prices for both you and your customers - if the items take you a long time to make, remember to factor in the cost of materials plus your time and skill going into them.

By staying creative and following the best practices for selling Macramé, you can make a living doing something you love. With the proper marketing and dedication to your craft, there is no limit to the success you can achieve with macramé.

Teaching Macramé Classes or Workshops

Another great way to make money with macramé is by teaching classes or workshops. With this business model, you can share your passion for macramé while helping others learn this rewarding craft. Not to mention, teaching classes is a great way to meet new people and build relationships with customers and clients.

Starting your own business is a great way to be your boss and make extra money.

And what better way to do that than by teaching macramé classes, seminars or workshops?

Before starting, you must create detailed lessons and projects plans for each class or workshop you intend to teach. These strategies will ensure that your students get the best possible educational experience and make the most of their time with you.

Whether you're leading in-person or virtual classes, there are plenty of ways to engage with students and ensure an enjoyable learning experience.

In a class setting, instructors can support their students through step-by-step tutorials and explain various techniques in detail. Teaching how to create specific projects is also an option — participants can take home their finished piece as a souvenir of their experience.

Workshops and seminars can be more focused and tailored toward experienced macramé artists looking for fresh ideas or want to refine certain skill sets. Providing demonstration pieces as references for new concepts can help encourage creative exploration.

Once you have created your lesson plans, it's time to start marketing your business. Create fliers, ads, and postings on social media to let others know about your services, as well as reach out directly to local craft stores, yarn shops, community centers, and bookstores about hosting your classes in their space.

With the right amount of preparation and dedication, teaching macramé can be an enjoyable experience for you and your students—plus a great source of income.

Whether running online or in-person classes, teaching macramé is fun and rewarding. Seeing your students' progress and joy when completing a project will be its reward and helping them learn this beloved craft is priceless.

Now that you know all about the different ways you can make money with macramé, it's time to start selling your skills and creations. You need basic supplies like rope or cord, scissors, and a few other household items to get started. Once your supplies are gathered, find inspiration for your first project by browsing Pinterest or Instagram. And before you know it, you'll be cranking out beautiful works of art—and making money while doing something you love.

With its easy learning curve and high-profit potential, there has never been a better time to get into macramé. Following the tips in this paragraph, you can start selling your creations in no time flat. So if you're looking for a creative and profitable way to make money, macramé is the perfect option.

Conclusion

Now that you know the basics of macramé, it's time to start creating your own unique and beautiful pieces. Don't be afraid to experiment with different shapes, sizes, and colors to find the perfect design for you. Have faith in yourself and don't give up. With dedication, trial and error, a bit of imagination, and the right amount of time - you will be astonished at what your hands can create with macramé. So go ahead and start knotting – the possibilities are endless.

Whether you're looking for a new way to decorate your home or just want something creative and fun to do, macramé is the perfect hobby. Plus, you don't need to buy any special equipment or tools; just some string and a little bit of patience and creativity.

So go ahead, grab some supplies, and start knotting. You won't believe the gorgeous art you can create with just a few materials and the basic knots you have found in this book.

Whether it's a wall hanging, plant hanger, or knotted jewelry, you're sure to find the perfect project for your needs.

Start your macramé journey today and show off your unique and creative artwork to friends and family.

Happy knotting!

Appendix

Basic Macramé Terms and Abbreviations

O f course, you could also expect specific terms you would be dealing with while trying macramé out. By knowing these terms, it would be easier for you to make macramé projects. You will not have a hard time, and the crafting would be a breeze!

For this, you could keep the following in mind!

Alternating

This is applied to patterns where more than one cord is being tied together. It involves switching and looping, just like the half-stitch.

Adjacent

These are knots or cords that rest following one another.

Bar

When a distinct area is raised in the pattern, it means that you have created a 'bar.' This could either be diagonal, horizontal, or vertical.

Band

It is a design that has been knotted to be flat or wide.

Buttonhole (BH)

This is another name given to the Crown or Lark's Head knot. It has been used since the Victorian Era.

Button Knot

This is a knot that is firm and round.

Bundle

These are cords that have been grouped as one. They could be held together by a knot.

Braided Cord

These are materials with individual fibers that are grouped as one. It is also more substantial than most materials because all the fibers work together as one.

Braid

Sometimes called a plate, this describes three or more cords that have been woven under or over each other.

Crook

This is just the part of the loop that has been curved and situated near the crossing point.

Core

This term refers to a group of cords that are running along the center of a knot. They are also called filling cords.

Chinese Crown Knot

This is usually used for Asian-inspired jewelry or décor.

Diameter

This describes the material's thickness based on millimeters.

Fringe

This technique allows cords to dangle down with individual fibers that unravel along the length of the pattern.

Findings

They are closures for necklaces, crimp beads, jump rings, clasps, wires, rings and even watches: everything you can add as final detail to make your designs complete. There are so many finishes, including Silver, Gold, Bronze, Antique Copper and more.

Gemstone Chips

This is the term given to semi-precious stones that are used to decorate or embellish your macramé projects. The best ones are usually quartz, jade, and turquoise.

Interlace

This is a pattern that could be woven or intertwined so that different areas could be linked together.

Micro-Macramé

This is the term given to relatively small Macramé projects. Micro-macramé is a type of miniature Macramé (so named to differentiate it from Classic Macramé, which allows you to create larger decorative items, such as rugs or pillows). It is a technique usually used for the creation of earrings, bracelets and other jewels where the different knots or chains of knots often alternate with beads and precious stones.

Mount

To mount or mounting means that you have to attach a cord to a frame, dowel, or ring. This is usually done at the start of a project.

Netting

This is a process of knotting that describes knots formed between open rows of space. It is usually used in wall hangings, curtains, and hammocks.

Picot

These are loops that go through the edge of what you have knotted.

Tension or Taut

This is the term given to holding cords that have been secured or pulled straight so that they would be tighter than the other working cords.

Working End

This is the part of the cord that is used to construct the knot.

Weave

This is the process of letting the cords move, as you let them pass over several segments in your pattern.

Regular Macramé Terms and Knot Abbreviations

Macramé examples and bunches are a moderate and straightforward art to learn. It requires not many devices and only some straightforward information on essential bunches. This guide shows you six regular macramé hitches that you'll have the option to use to make an assortment of macramé projects.

Here are a couple of terms that you need to know before you begin:

- **Hitching rope.** This is the line or set of ropes used to make the bunch for some random join.
- **Bunch-bearing rope.** This is the line or set of strings that the hitching lines are folded over. The hitching line and bunch-bearing string can change from step to step in a macramé design. For instance, when you work the corner-to-corner half hitch (appeared underneath), you will have one bunch bearing string, yet there will be various tying ropes worked in a steady progression on that equivalent bunch bearing line.
- **Working Cord**: This is the string or bundle of strings that you use to make the actual knots.
- **Filler or Holding Cord**: This is the string or set of strings that your knots wrap around.
- **Sennit.** This indicates to a cluster of knots or set of knots that are worked in repeat. For instance, if you work six half knot lines in succession, at that point, you have a sennit of 6 half knots.

Macrame Knot Abbreviations

LHK: Larks Head Knot

SK: Square Knot

HK: Half Knot

ASK: Alternating Square Knot

SHH: Single Half Hitch (first half of a double half hitch)

DHH: Double Half Hitch

THH: Triple Half Hitch (each cord is knotted onto the Holding Cord 3 times)

OK: Overhand Knot

ASHH: Alternating Single Half Hitch Chain

BK: Berry Knot

CCK: Chinese Crown Knot

JK: Josephine Knot

Macrame Term Abbreviations

WC – Working Cord

HC – Holding or Filler Cord

Made in United States
Troutdale, OR
02/19/2024

17803248R00075